10 Steps to Starter

Legal Protections and Operational Strategies Every New Business Needs

Sydnee R. Mack, Esq.

Sydnee Mack Attorney at Law LLC
Atlanta, GA

Cover Art/Design By:
Mackenzie N. Mack

Syd Mack Media created this publication to provide you with accurate and authoritative information concerning the subject matter covered. However, Syd Mack Media does not render legal or other professional advice, and this publication is not a substitute for the advice of an attorney. If you require legal or other expert advice, you should seek the services of a competent attorney or other professional.

I would like to dedicate this book to my mother, Dr. Jean Jackson, my first and most courageous hero.

TABLE OF CONTENTS

STEP 1

GET YOUR MIND RIGHT:

PREPARING FOR THE RIDE OF YOUR LIFE

Look, it's 2018. Everybody wants to start a business, a side-hustle, a blog or whatever. If you're reading this book, that means one of two things: (1) you're one of my close friends or family and you really love me and want to support me (I love you too boo!!); or (2) you are serious about your business and you want to get it started the right way. Whether you fall into the first or second category (or maybe both), by reading this book, you are taking a great first step towards getting your business off on the right foot.

Ten Steps to StartUP was designed to: 1) help you navigate the challenges and 2) answer some of the legal questions you will have as you start your business. As a business lawyer and law firm owner, I have worked with many different businesses from the dude trying to monetize his YouTube® Channel to multi-million-dollar corporations. As a result of my experience, I have come across lots of questions about how to start a business that is compliant with the law, regulations and industry best practices. This book is my answer to all of those questions. It is designed to be a valuable guide that will equip you with the basic knowledge, tools and resources that all new business owners should have.

However, be warned! This book is NOT, I repeat, NOT a replacement for having a knowledgeable, experienced lawyer who will not only answer specific questions relating to your business, but also perform the work necessary to get your small business legally compliant from its inception.

Before we jump into the meat of this thing, there is one important piece of information that you should know before starting a business: it's really, really hard! Starting a business is one of the toughest, most courageous things you will ever do, besides maybe having children. Unless you have a puppy. Because let's face it, puppies are a lot of work!

This life that you have chosen is not always glamorous, and the road to success will never be what you imagined it to be. You will hit roadblocks, potholes, unsupportive friends, family members or ex-lovers named Tyrone (yes, I'm talking to you, and yes, we have all had a Tyrone). You will have days where you are hoping the phone rings just once because it hasn't all week; when you are trying to decide whether to put gas in your car or invest in your business; when you are discouraged because the words you slaved years to write, someone copied and reposted on their blog in seconds. When those days come (and they will come if they haven't already), I want you to open this book, and read this message:

I know it's hard. I know you're tired. I know you feel like giving up. I know you just want to curl up in a ball and cry. I know some days you feel lost. I know you want to surf the job boards and find a job. I know you just wish it could be different. I know you wish it could be easy. But don't give up, just hold on. Because if it were easy, everyone would be doing it. The journey to entrepreneurship can be so bitter, but the rewards so sweet. Those rewards may not come quickly, but I promise they will come…just hold on.

STEP 2

GET STARTED:

BUSINESS PLANS AND NDA'S

Section 2.1 The Business Plan

Ok listen, every business started as an idea. So, if an idea is all you've got at this point, then you're right on track! How do you turn your idea, hobby, passion …etc. into a business? Now, if I knew the answer to that question, I would be on a yacht somewhere sipping tea and eating crumpets. But alas, I am here writing this book eating cashews dreaming about all of the tea and crumpets I will eat someday…. and yes, I will be eating them! While I can't tell you how to take your idea and turn it into a full-blown business, I can tell you that every great business starts with a plan. Someone once told me that the difference between a business and a hobby is that one makes money and one doesn't. That is only partially true. There are hundreds of businesses out there not making any money. But every business has a viable *plan* to make money. To help you develop a strategy to turn your hobby into a profitable business, I've developed some questions you should be able to answer. Give it a shot!

Get Started Quiz

- What is the product or service?
- What problem will your product/service solve?
- How is your product/service different from similar products/services?
- How much will it cost to develop your product?
- How will you fund your business?
    - Grants
    - Loans
    - Line of credit (credit card)
    - Personal Cash
    - Investors
    - Partners
- Can you manage the operations of the business alone or do you need help?
- Where will your business live? (online, at home, brick and mortar…etc.)

- Does your state, county or municipality require special and/or general licensing to run this kind of business?
- Do you need any classes, degrees or certifications to provide your services? If so, how much will it cost?
- How much will you charge for your products/services?
- Are your goods/services priced competitively for the market but also at a point that will yield a reasonable profit?
- Who is your target customer?
- How do you plan to reach your target customer?
- If you have a product, how will you distribute it?
- If your business takes 6-12 months to turn a profit, can you afford to pay your bills with little to no income?
- How do you plan to grow your business after year(s) one, three, five and ten?

If that felt like a fun exercise, it's probably because you had the answers to the questions. If that felt like a pop quiz worth 50% of your final grade that you had no idea was coming and hadn't prepared for, that probably means you need to sit down and take some time to prepare thoughtful answers to those questions. Answering those questions will help you focus your thoughts and develop a plan for your business. In addition to the list of questions above, I have compiled a checklist below of some important things that you will need to get your business started. Please note: this is a general list that may vary depending on the type of entity you've selected. #yourewelcome

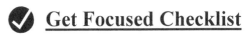

Get Focused Checklist

☐ Choose a name for your business

☐ Decide which state your business will be located (usually, the state where you live and/or do the most business)

☐ Select/Appoint a registered agent (a person registered in the same state as the business who is designated to receive service and other official communications on behalf of the company)

☐ Select an address for the business (if you register your business using a home address, you can use a mailing address for your website, business cards and other marketing materials)

Pro Tip: If you use a P.O. Box for your mailing address, you can use the street address of the post office or UPS location for your marketing materials. That way, it looks like you have a physical address vs. a post office box.

☐ Register your business with the Secretary of State

☐ Get an Employer Identification Number (EIN)

☐ Establish company by-laws (applicable for corporations including nonprofit corporations) or execute an operating agreement (applicable for limited liability companies)

☐ Check to see if your state requires your business to have a Sales/Use Tax Certificate

☐ Obtain a business license (if necessary) with your state, county, city and/or municipality

☐ Obtain business insurance (you may need one, some or none of the following: general liability, hazard, errors & omissions (E&O), accident, professional liability)

☐ Develop a purpose statement (a brief description of your products/services and value proposition) for public relations and marketing purposes

☐ Obtain personal health insurance

☐ Open a company bank account

☐ Get a business telephone number

☐ Get a business email address

☐ Establish business pages for social media (Facebook, Twitter, Instagram, LinkedIn, Snapchat etc.)

☐ Set up payment processing (PayPal, Square etc.)

☐ Prepare a calendar of all important events

☐ Develop a system for keeping track of income and

expenses (QuickBooks, excel spreadsheet, accountant)

☐ Design a logo

☐ Create business cards

☐ Identify key partners (distributors, wholesalers, manufacturers, couriers etc.)

Section 2.2 Non-Disclosure Agreements

So, you've got your game plan together and now you need to engage potential partners, investors, manufacturers, developers, employees...etc. about your idea. How do you communicate your idea to these key people without fear of them spilling the beans before you're ready? Make them sign a non-disclosure agreement. A non-disclosure agreement is a legally binding contract between two or more parties where one or all parties agree not to share confidential information with other parties, as specified in the agreement. Companies often use these agreements to protect confidential or proprietary information that is crucial to the commercial success of their business. They can be stand-alone agreements or provisions of larger more complex agreements, like employment agreements, independent contractor agreements and manufacturing agreements.

Whether you are engaging someone for the first time and need to execute a stand-alone agreement or plan to include a non-disclosure provision in one of your standard agreements, the following are some important tips for drafting, reviewing and executing effective non-disclosure agreements:

1. **KEEP YOUR MOUTH CLOSED**. Make sure to have the agreement signed and in place BEFORE disclosing any confidential information. I know that you are bursting with excitement and ready to tell every person you meet about your fabulous new idea, but in the interest of self-preservation, hold tight! Any information you disclose prior to executing the non-disclosure may not be protected, especially if the person you blabbed to discloses to a third party before you can get a formal agreement in place. If you slip up and tell before you have a non-disclosure in place, make sure your agreement includes previously disclosed information.

2. **CLEARLY DEFINE CONFIDENTIAL**. Make sure your non-disclosure is specific and includes ALL the information you want to protect from exposure. You cannot protect every single piece of information you have, but you can protect any information that, if released, would be detrimental to the success of your business.

   Picture This: The following is a sample definition of confidential information that you may consider including in your pre-business launch confidentiality agreement:

"For the purposes of this Agreement, **"Confidential Information"** means any information not generally known to the public or recognized as standard industry practice, including but not limited to [any data; reports; studies; interpretations; forecasts; know-how; compositions; plans; strategies; strategic partnerships and the existence of the discussions between the Parties; employee information; financial records and inventory records of the Company; intellectual property; trade secrets; product development plans; research; ideas; concepts; designs; formulas; technology; devices; inventions; methods or processes, whether or not patented or patentable; the substance of agreements with clients, suppliers and any third party; customer

> lists; supplier lists; marketing arrangements; channels of distribution; pricing policies and records and any such other information normally understood to be confidential or otherwise designated as such in writing by the disclosing party."

This definition may be applicable to your business, but it may not be. Be sure to tailor your definition of "confidential information" to suit your specific needs.

3. **INCLUDE ALL AFFILIATES**. Most people in business do not work alone. They usually work with a team. In order to make a decision about whether to do business with you, the non-disclosing party may have to share the information covered by the non-disclosure agreement with key stakeholders of their business including but not limited to: lawyers, accountants, tax advisors, agents, assignees, employees...etc. You also may need to execute separate agreements with those people to ensure their compliance.

4. **GET YOUR INFO BACK**. If you have to turn over documents, formulas, PowerPoint decks, etc., make sure your contract clearly states that ALL information given to the receiving party will be returned to its rightful owner. Also, make sure to include a deadline by which the information must be returned. If you don't want the information back, you can alternatively demand that it be destroyed.

5. **SET A TIMELINE**. Nothing lasts forever, and neither should your non-disclosure agreement. Make sure to clearly outline how long the information should be kept confidential.

STEP 3

GET IT TOGETHER:

SELECTING A BUSINESS ENTITY

Once you've decided on a name, a logo, a marketing plan and a plan to generate revenue, it's time to GET YOUR BUSINESS TOGETHER by turning your idea, plan, good or service into a formal state and/or federally recognized entity. But what kind of business (entity) is right for you and your organization? This chapter will compare the most common entity types by describing the general characteristics of each type including: formation, ownership, control, owner liability and tax liability. The entity types listed in this book are not exhaustive. Meaning, there are other entity-types that prospective business owners can choose from, but I won't be discussing them here. You'll have to find another book/app for those…sorry.

Further, this section only addresses some general aspects of US federal income tax law, but the tax consequences of selecting an entity are complex and can vary depending on the type of business, the type of owners, applicable state tax laws and other circumstances. For more information on state and/or federal income tax classification rules for corporations, LLCs and partnerships, be sure to consult with an accountant.

Section 3.1 Sole Proprietorships
What is it?

A sole proprietorship is a business owned by one person with no formal legal structure or status separate from its owner. Essentially, the business is the owner and the owner is the business.

Who owns it?

One individual person. The defining characteristic of a *sole* proprietorship is that it is owned by one person. Most sole proprietorships are also "one-man bands" in that owners are the sole employee of the business. But, that doesn't have to be the case. Sole proprietors can employ millions of people just as long as none of said employees have an ownership interest in the business.

Who Manages it?

A sole proprietorship is managed by the owner.

Who is liable for it?

The owner of the business is liable for ALL activities of the business... the good, the bad and the ugly.

How is it taxed?

The same as the individual. The sole proprietor taxpayer generally attaches an addendum to his/her personal tax return outlining the transactions of the business. The net profit or loss shown on the addendum is then transferred to the sole proprietor's tax return and included as income.

How to get it started?

Start doing business. There is no formal process to getting a sole proprietorship started.

Benefits

The major benefit of starting a sole proprietorship is that there is no formal process to getting started. There are no filings that need to be done and no fees to be paid. Just start doing business. For example, as a sole proprietor, if you want to set up a lemonade stand on the corner, then set up your stand and start doing business. Unless of course, you need a permit or license or something, but that's a conversation for another day.

Disadvantages

There is no legal protection for the owner of a sole proprietor. Because you are the business, the business' debts, liabilities, lawsuits etc., are your debts, liabilities and lawsuits and vice versa. So, if the business gets sued, you get sued. Conversely, if you get sued, the person who is suing you can attack your business as well.

Section 3.2 Partnerships
What is it?

There are many kinds of partnerships, but I am referring to the "general partnership." A partnership is an association of two or more people who act as co-owners of a business for profit. Each partner must contribute something to the partnership, whether it be money, skills, expertise, or resources.

Who owns it?

A partnership is owned by its partners. By definition, you must have at least two partners to form a partnership. There are no solos in partnership.

Who manages it?

The partners are responsible for managing the partnership.

Who is liable for it?

Each partner has unlimited personal liability. If the partnership is sued or goes into debt, all partners are responsible for the full amount of the debt. For example, if a company is owned by two partners and one partner takes out a $100,000 loan, the other partner is also responsible for paying back the full loan amount of $100,000.

How is it taxed?

Unless otherwise agreed to in writing, each

partner generally shares equally in the profits/losses of the business. Like sole proprietorships, profits and losses from the business flow through the business directly to the partners. Each partner is responsible for filing his/her own taxes and must include income from the partnership in his/her individual tax return.

How to get it started?

There is no formal process to forming a partnership. If two or more people get together and decide that they want to do business together, a partnership is formed. The laws have default rules to govern partnerships in the absence of any formal arrangement, but all partnerships should formalize their business relationship through a partnership agreement.

Benefits

There are hardly any corporate formalities that must be observed by partnerships making them easy to form and relatively easy to dissolve.

Disadvantages

Partnerships have very few formalities that they

must observe. It is the sole responsibility of the partners to provide structure and regulation for their business. If the partners are diligent and responsible, this shouldn't be a problem. But if they're not, it could start to feel more like a marriage than a business (and not in a good way). Another huge drawback of partnerships is that there is no protection from personal liability for the partners.

<u>Section 3.3 Limited Liability Companies</u>
What is it?

A Limited Liability Company (LLC) is a business entity that stands alone separate and apart from its owners and provides owners with protection from personal liability as well as the debts and other obligations of the company. The term "limited liability" means that there is a limitation on the amount an owner can lose resulting from a lawsuit or other loss suffered by the company. The liability for losses is limited to the amount of the owner's investment in the business.

Who owns it?

Owners of an LLC are called members. A single person can form an LLC. There is no minimum number of members required to form an LLC.

Who manages it?

The member(s) is/are responsible for managing an LLC.

Who is liable for it?

The LLC is liable for its own debts and liabilities thus providing members with a shield from personal liability, as long as members maintain personal assets and liabilities separate from business assets and liabilities.

How is it taxed?

While LLCs limit personal liability for their owners, similar to the protections from liability afforded corporations, LLCs are subject to single or pass through taxation, like partnerships. For example, all profits generated from the business flow through the company and pass directly to its members. Members are then responsible for paying personal income taxes on all funds received from the business.

Multimember LLCs are automatically treated as partnerships for tax purposes. However, multimember

LLCs can elect to be taxed as S-Corps but must file a form with the IRS to formally make said election.

How to get it started?

An LLC is formed by filing articles of organization with the Secretary of State, appointing a registered agent and paying a fee. Most states have general articles that you can use so you won't have to draft your own. You will also need to get an Employment Identification Number (EIN) from the IRS. Individual states may have additional requirements for LLC formation. Check with your local Secretary of State for additional requirements.

Benefits

LLCs provide their owners with strong protection from potential liability (much like corporations) but are not required to observe certain formalities that corporations do, such as: holding board meetings, drafting meeting minutes and maintaining proper meeting records. LLC members also have the freedom to govern the business however they deem fit. For these reasons, LLCs are my recommended entity choice for small businesses.

It's like Corporation Lite, all the fun of corporations with none of the extra headache. And, if you decide at a later time that you would like to re-form your business as a corporation, you can.

Disadvantages

There really aren't many disadvantages to forming an LLC. However, LLCs cannot issue stock. As a result, they miss a key opportunity to raise capital for the business. Corporations also receive generous tax breaks that individuals and pass-through entities (LLCs, partnerships and sole proprietorships) do not. Depending on how much money the company makes, it may be more advantageous for it to be taxed as a corporation versus an LLC. This is generally only true for businesses that make A LOT of money (I'm talking millions of dollars).

Section 3.4 Corporations

All for-profit corporations (and even nonprofit corporations) share many similarities, like how they are formed, who owns them and who governs them. However, there are some slight differences that are important to note regarding how they are taxed and limitations on ownership.

C-Corporations
What is it?

A corporation is a stand-alone legal entity that exists separate and apart from the individual or individuals who own it. As its own entity, C-corps can own and sell property and other assets; sue and be sued; and exercise other powers granted to it by law, the same as a natural person. Think of it like this, creating a corporation is essentially like creating a brand-new person.

Who owns it?

A corporation is owned by shareholders (also referred to as stockholders). Shareholders own shares of stock which are units of ownership. The more shares of stock a shareholder owns, the greater the stake or share of interest he/she has in the corporation. There are no limits on the number or classes of stock that a C-Corp can issue. There are also no limitations on who can hold stock in a C-Corp. Shareholders can be actual people, companies, trusts, estates or any entity that can own property.

Who Manages it?

C-Corporations are managed by a board of directors who are elected by the shareholders. The board is responsible for electing officers who are responsible for managing the day-to-day operations of the business.

Who is liable for it?

A C-Corp is liable for its own acts, omissions, debts and liabilities. Because corporations are stand-alone entities, shareholders and directors enjoy a strong shield from personal liability for the actions of the corporation as well as any actions they perform during their employment/relationship with the corporation.

How is it taxed?

The profit generated by companies is taxed twice: once at the corporate level and again at the shareholder level. Corporations, much like individuals, are responsible for paying taxes on their income. This is the first level of taxation. Then, if the corporation make a profit, it must distribute the profits of the business (dividends) to its shareholders. These profit distributions are considered income for the individual shareholders and they will have to include it as income on their individual tax returns. This is the second level of taxation.

How to get it started?

Every state has its own laws governing corporations, but generally, you form a corporation by: (a) filing articles of incorporation with the Secretary of State; (b) appointing a registered agent; (c) paying a fee and (d) applying for an Employer Identification Number (EIN) with the IRS. However, to finalize the formation of a corporation, you must hold an organizational meeting of the initial board of directors where you should: (1) adopt corporate by-laws (an internal document that governs the corporation); (2) elect members of the board; (3) appoint officers of the board and (4) approve the issuance of stock. If you can't hold a meeting, you can also accomplish the aforementioned tasks by obtaining signed, written consent from all initial directors of the corporation.

Benefits

As a business structure, corporations provide the most protection from liability for their directors and shareholders. They can also offer stock as a perk or benefit to employees and potential investors as well as a means of raising capital. This business structure is ideal for large companies with lots of cash.

Disadvantages

Of all the business entity types, corporations are generally the most difficult to establish and maintain. For example, issuing and distributing shares of stock can be a very complicated process, especially if you are dealing with several different classes and large numbers of shares. You should always consult with both a lawyer and an accountant/bookkeeper before attempting to issue any shares of stock. Further, maintaining a corporation requires adherence to strict corporate formalities which include holding regular meetings and maintaining all monies, contracts, accounts…etc., of the business separate from that of any of its shareholders. Adhering to corporate formality and maintaining the autonomous integrity of the business is important because it is what shields shareholders, directors and employees from personal liability. It's also very tedious. And did I mention the part about being taxed twice on the same money?

S-Corporations

What is it?

An S-Corp shares many similarities to a C-Corp. There are only several slight differences, as noted below. Accordingly, an S-Corp is a stand-alone legal entity that exists separate and apart from the individual or individuals who own it. As its own entity, corporations can own and sell property and other assets; sue and be sued; and exercise other powers granted to it by law, the same as a natural person.

Who owns it?

An S-Corp is owned by shareholders (also referred to as stockholders). However, S-Corps are strictly for small corporations and the number of shareholders is limited to 100 or less. There are also limits on *who* can own S-Corp stock. Only people, estates and some trusts can own S-Corp stock.

Who Manages it?

S-Corps are managed by a board of directors who are elected by the shareholders. The board is responsible for electing officers who are responsible for managing the day-to-day operations of the company.

Who is liable for it?

An S-Corp is liable for its own acts, omissions, debts and liabilities. Because S-corps are stand-alone entities, shareholders and directors enjoy a strong shield from personal liability for the actions of the corporation as well as any actions they perform during their employment/relationship with the corporation.

How is it taxed?

The taxation of an S-Corp is very similar to that of a limited liability company in that the business does not pay tax on the profits. Only the shareholders pay taxes for dividends received from the corporation. This is what is called a pass or flow through taxation because the profits pass through the corporation directly to the shareholders.

How to get it started?

Every state has its own laws governing corporations, but generally, you form a corporation by: (1) filing articles of incorporation with the Secretary of State; (2) appointing a registered agent; (3) paying a fee and (4) applying for an Employer Identification Number with the IRS. However, to finalize the formation of an S-Corp, you must hold an organizational meeting of the initial board of directors where you should: (a) adopt corporate by-laws (an internal document that governs the corporation); (b) elect members of the board; (c) appoint officers of the board and (d) approve the issuance of stock. If you can't hold a meeting, you can also accomplish the aforementioned tasks by obtaining signed, written consent from all initial directors of the corporation.

Benefits

Similar to C-Corps, S-Corps provide maximum protection from liability for their directors and shareholders. S-Corps are also not subject to double taxation as C-Corps are.

Disadvantages

S-Corps have disadvantages similar to that of C-Corps in that they are the most difficult to establish and maintain. For example, issuing and distributing stock can be a very complicated process, especially if you are dealing with several different classes of shares and large numbers of shares. You should always consult with both a lawyer and an accountant/bookkeeper before attempting to issue any shares of stock. Further, maintaining a corporation requires adherence to strict corporate formalities which include holding regular meetings and keeping all monies, contracts, accounts...etc., of the business separate from that of any of its shareholders. Adhering to corporate formality and maintaining the autonomous integrity of the business is important because it helps to shield shareholders, directors and employees from personal liability.

Nonprofit Corporations
What is it?

A 501(c)3 nonprofit corporation is an incorporated organization that's purpose is "religious, charitable, scientific, testing for public safety, literary, or educational purposes, or to foster national or international amateur sports competition (but only if no part of its activities involve the provision of athletic facilities or equipment), or for the prevention of cruelty to children or animals." You may already know this, but there are several kinds of charitable organizations governed by various Sections of the Internal Revenue Code. However, this book will only discuss nonprofits governed by Section 501(c)3.

Who owns it?

No one can own a nonprofit. Because the purpose of a nonprofit is to fulfill a charitable purpose versus to turn a profit, there is no need for ownership. But, just because the goal of a nonprofit is not to make a profit, there is nothing that forbids it from earning income that exceeds its operating expenses. If a nonprofit does experience a surplus, it has to reinvest the money back into the business instead of distributing profits to directors or officers.

Who manages it?

Nonprofits, like other corporations, are managed by a board of directors who appoint officers to manage the day-to-day operations of the business.

Who is liable for it?

Like other corporations, nonprofit officers and directors receive strong protections from personal liability.

Accordingly, the nonprofit is liable for its own acts, omissions, debts and liabilities. Because corporations are stand-alone entities, nonprofit directors and officers enjoy a strong shield from personal liability for the actions of the corporation as well as any actions they perform during their employment/relationship with the corporation.

How is it taxed?

Duh, they're not! 501(c)3 nonprofits enjoy an exemption from taxes due to their charitable nature. To incentivize charitable works/giving, the government allows 501(c)3 organizations to conduct business tax-free.

How to get it started?

The process of getting a nonprofit started can be long and tedious. Here is a list of all the things you need to do to get your nonprofit started (in no particular order):

- File Federal Income Tax Exemption Form
- File State Income Tax Exemption Form
- File articles of incorporation with the Secretary of State
- Appoint a registered agent
- Secure Tax/EIN Number

- File Notice of Publication
- Draft Nonprofit Bylaws
- Hold Initial Board of Directors Meeting

Benefits

One of the major benefits of a nonprofit is that it operates tax-free. It also provides tax breaks for donors/contributors. This entity-type is best if you want to secure capital for the business through fundraising to provide charitable service(s) to others at low or no cost to them. The charitable nature of the business also does not prevent you from charging for goods/services to help pay for expenses.

Disadvantages

The biggest disadvantage of a nonprofit is …well you guessed it! There are no profits from the business that can be passed on to owners through distributions. Lack of "profits," however, does not mean there is not BIG money to be made in the nonprofit business. Plenty of nonprofit CEOs make million-dollar+ salaries. But, because no one can own a nonprofit, your salary and any other monies you receive are at the sole discretion of the board. Another disadvantage is that you cannot (by yourself) control a nonprofit. Even if you founded the organization, you are still subject to the mandates of the board. Nonprofits must also observe a ton of corporate formalities, similar to other corporations.

 <u>Just So You Know</u>:

Most new businesses should select LLC as their business entity of choice. Limited liability corporations provide the best of both worlds in that they provide owners with the limited liability protections of corporations as well as the flexibility and informality of partnerships.

Entity Type	Who Owns?	Who Manages?	Who is Liable?	Taxation	Getting Started	Pros	Cons
Sole Proprietorship	Owned by one person	Owner	Owner	Owner is responsible for paying taxes on net income of the business	No formal requirements	No corporate formalities for getting started.	No protections from personal liability
Single Member LLC	A single member	The Managing Member	The LLC as, long as business is kept separate from owner	Profits flow through the business to the member as personal income	File Articles of Organization + Filing Fee* + EIN	Limited formality for establishment and maintenance. Shielded from personal liability	Cannot issue stock. Enjoy less tax breaks than corporations.
Multi Member LLC	Two or more members	The Members	The LLC as, long as business is kept separate from owners	Profits flow through the business to the members as personal income	File Articles of Organization + Filing Fee* + EIN	Limited formality for establishment and maintenance. Shielded from personal liability	Cannot issue stock. Enjoy less tax breaks than corporations.
C-Corp	Shareholders (unlimited number)	Board of Directors	The corporation as, long as corporate formality is observed	The corporation pays taxes and shareholders pay taxes individually on dividends received	File Articles of Incorporation + Registered Agent + Filing Fee + EIN	Strong protection from personal liability	Lots of corporate formalities to observe. Difficult to establish and maintain.
S-Corp	Shareholders (no more than 100)	Board of Directors	The corporation as, long as corporate formality is observed	Profits flow through the business to the partners as personal income	File Articles of Incorporation + Registered Agent + Filing Fee + EIN	Strong protection from personal liability	Lots of corporate formalities to observe. Difficult to establish and maintain.
Non-Profit Corporation	No one	Board of Directors	The corporation as, long as corporate	N/A	Federal tax exemption application, state tax exemption Secretary of State, filing fees, EIN Number, Publish Notice of Incorporation, Draft Bylaws	Can raise funds. Are exempt from paying taxes	Cannot own it, so you cannot control it. No profits.
Partnership	partners	partners	partners	Profits flow through the business to the partners as personal income	No Formal Requirements	Easy to form, easy to dissolve	No protection from personal liability for partners

STEP 4

GET IT ON PAPER:

OPERATING AGREEMENTS, BYLAWS AND PARTNERSHIP AGREEMENTS

If you plan to own your business with other people, it is imperative to put your ownership terms on paper. An ownership agreement can be an operating agreement, bylaws or a partnership agreement, depending upon the kind of business you have. Your agreement should answer questions like: "How will we break a tie if we don't agree on something?" "What portion of the losses will I be expected to cover if we go into debt?" Or my personal favorite, "I hate you, and I want out. How do I sell my half of this thing?" This chapter will provide guidance on how to answer those questions by explaining the different kinds of ownership agreements and highlighting terms that you should consider including in them.

Owning a business with others is a lot like a marriage. When things are good, they're great. When they're bad, they can get ugly. Think of an ownership agreement as your business pre-nup. It will not only help you to govern your business while it's good but also help you to navigate the challenges of business when and if things go bad. Similar to a pre-nup, it is best for each owner to have his/her OWN attorney review the agreement prior to signing. Think about it. Would you sign a pre-nup drafted, reviewed and explained to you by your future spouse's lawyer? Me either. Be sure to make sure your individual interests are represented by hiring your own lawyer.

Wait, one last thing about ownership agreements before we delve deeper into the different kinds and important provisions. While ownership agreements are important, they are not necessarily required. In the absence of a formal written agreement, states have laws that govern disputes that arise amongst business owners. However, rather than allowing the state to dictate the resolution of your issues, put your wishes on paper so that you and your co-owners can retain maximum control when it comes to making decisions for your company. And remember, even with an operating agreement, bylaws or partnership agreement, your business is still subject to the laws/regulations of your state. Make sure to visit your state's Secretary of State website to determine what laws and/or regulations may apply to your business.

Section 4.1 Operating Agreements and LLCs

An operating agreement is a legal document that outlines the ownership interests and duties of members of limited liability companies (LLCs) and cannot be used in connection with any other type of business entity. It also defines the company's management structure, describes how the company's profits/losses are allocated and distributed, and sets out the terms of engagement for the company's members. Single Member LLCs can execute operating agreements; however, it is most important to implement operating agreements for multi-member LLCs (an LLC with two or more members). Every operating agreement will be different based on the unique desires and needs of each LLC and its members; but, the following are some of the basic provisions that should be covered by every operating agreement.

Members and Membership Interests

Operating agreements should include the names and addresses of each of the current members of the LLC. It can also include other contact information for each member such as phone numbers and email addresses, but names and addresses are required at a minimum. This information is generally placed in an attachment to the original document called a schedule, appendix or exhibit.

The schedule containing the names and addresses of each of the members should also include the ownership interests of each of the members. An ownership interest is the percentage of the company owned by each member. The percentage of the company owned by each member is at the discretion of the members and is usually equal to the amount of money invested into the LLC by each member (unless stated otherwise in the operating agreement). Profits and losses will also be allocated according to ownership interest unless otherwise stated in the ownership agreement.

Capital Contribution

The amount invested in the company by each member is referred to as a capital contribution. This initial investment can be made in the form of cash or other assets of value such as real property or shares of stock from a corporation. Capital contributions are an important fundraising mechanism for LLCs. It is how most LLCs fund day-to-day operations until the company turns a profit.

In an operating agreement, the capital contribution provision should specify not only the initial contributions of members, but also expectations for future contributions; how and when requests can be made for additional capital contributions; the manner in which members can loan capital to the business; and consequences for failing to contribute required capital to the business.

Voting Rights

LLC members will often be forced to make difficult decisions regarding the management of the company such as adding or removing members, purchasing assets, holding meetings and incurring debt. The most democratic way to resolve any discrepancies is to put them to a vote of the members. To ensure that votes are conducted fairly and civilly, operating agreements should include voting provisions that set forth rules for voting.

The agreement should state the voting rights of each member (maybe some members won't have the right to vote) and what percentage of the membership vote is required to pass a resolution (i.e., majority: 51+% or unanimous: 100% of the vote). If there is an even number of members (i.e., two, four or six...etc. members) who share an interest in the company equally (50/50 or 25/25/25/25 ...etc.), also make sure to state which member will have the deciding vote in the event of a tie.

The agreement should also set forth different voting requirements for various kinds of actions to be taken by the company. For example, larger decisions like removal of a manager may require a unanimous or 100% vote whereas smaller decisions like office location may only require a majority (greater than 50%) vote.

Management

All members can manage the LLC equally if they wish but, it is more common for members to appoint one or more managers to oversee the day-to-day operations of the business. The operating agreement should outline the process for appointing manager(s) as well as the compensation, authority, role(s) and responsibilities of the manager(s). It should also describe the process for removing or replacing managers and whether or not the manager has to be a member of the LLC. Some states require the manager to be a member (or owner) of the business. Be sure to check with your state laws before appointing a manager.

Operating Agreement Hypo

To illustrate how membership interests, capital contributions and voting rights work, let's work through an illustrative, hypothetical (hypo) situation.

My friends, Ren, Stimpy and I decide to start an LLC that we wish to own equally with equal voting rights and execute an operating agreement stating the same. We decide that we need $300,000 to start our LLC. In order to raise this money, we agree that each of us will contribute 1/3 of the $300k necessary to start the business.

Accordingly, each of us will have to contribute $100,000 in cash or other assets to each own a thirty-three percent (33%) stake as equal owners of the company. Ren and I both have $100,000 in cash and we write checks made out to the LLC in the amount of $100,000 as our capital contributions.

However, Stimpy does not have cash. He has a $100,000 condo that he wishes to assign to the LLC as his capital contribution. Can Stimpy do this? Yes, he can. As long as the fair market value of the condo is $100,000, Stimpy can assign his interest in the condo over to the LLC as his capital contribution.

I then propose that we take out a loan to purchase office space for the business, but Ren disagrees. We therefore, must put the decision to a vote. Because we all own the business equally, with equal voting rights, we each have one vote to contribute to the decision-making of the company. Since Ren and I disagree, the deciding vote will be left with Stimpy. If the company only consisted of Ren and me, our operating agreement would designate which of us would get to make the final decision in the event of a split vote.

Does it all make sense now? If not, it may be time to lawyer up.

Transfer of Ownership Interests

A transfer of ownership interest is the sale, conveyance, assignment, transfer, pledge, grant of a security interest in or otherwise disposition of all or part of a member's ownership in the LLC. This provision not only outlines the terms under which a member can sell, convey or transfer his ownership interest in the LLC, but also to whom those interests can be transferred to. Most operating agreements give the non-transferring members the first opportunity to buy the transferring member's interest in the company through a provision called a "right of first refusal." This provision will become especially important in the event of the death or incapacity of a member. Without a carefully drafted transfer of ownership provision, a member's ownership interest will transfer through the state laws of intestacy, a will or trust. Be sure to structure this section of the operating agreement in a way that allows for non-transferring members to have a say in where the transferring members' interest is transferred, in the event of a member's death or incapacity.

Dissolution and Winding Up

Dissolution and winding up are fancy ways of saying "shutting down" and "tying up loose ends." An LLC may be dissolved for many reasons including but not limited to: a sale of all of the company's assets, written consent of all the members, court-ordered dissolution by a judge (usually in bankruptcy) and/or expiration of the operating agreement or other formation documents. The operating agreement can outline what other events, if any, may be grounds for dissolution of the company. It should also outline how the debts, liabilities, obligations, profits and assets will be settled during a process called "winding up." You do not have to wind up the business prior to dissolving it. If circumstances require you to dissolve the company immediately, you can do so and wind the affairs of the business up after.

Section 4.2 Bylaws and Corporations

Bylaws set forth the governance rules for corporations, including but not limited to: S-Corporations, C-Corporations and even nonprofit corporations. Because corporations rely heavily on adherence to corporate formalities to maintain their limited liability status, it is extremely important to implement strong bylaws to ensure proper procedure is followed to protect shareholders, the board of directors and officers from potential liability. In the absence of bylaws, a company will be subject to the default laws set forth by the State. The following are some of the important provisions that should be included in a corporation's bylaws.

Offices

This Section should state the name, state of incorporation and principal place of business (address) of the corporation. The information listed in this section should be the same as listed in the articles of incorporation that were filed with the Secretary of State. This is also the information that should be listed on any contracts entered into by the corporation.

Stockholders

Stockholders are the owners of a corporation. The role of the stockholders is to elect and remove directors from the board and approve fundamental corporate changes. An example of a fundamental corporate change is the sale of the assets of the corporation, the acquisition of another company or the merger of the corporation with another. The stockholder section of your agreement should cover the following:

- Meeting Requirements
  - Date/place of the Annual Meeting
  - Rules for Special Meetings
  - How notice of meetings will be disseminated
  - The minimum number of shareholders required to be present at each meeting (generally a majority of the shareholders with voting powers)
- Preparation of a list of stockholders
- Rules of conduct for meetings
- Voting Proxies (the ability to have someone else vote in a voting shareholder's absence)
- Actions that can be taken with written consent of all shareholders in lieu of a meeting
- Maintenance of records including record books, stock certificates, minute books and ledgers.

Board of Directors

A corporation's board of directors is responsible for

the management of the company as well as the election of its officers which includes high-level executives like the Chief President, Vice President, Treasurer and Corporate Secretary. The board must also, as one of its first acts, adopt the bylaws of the company. The bylaws cannot go into effect until the board votes to put them in to place. The following are important provisions that should be included in the provision governing the actions of the board.

- Powers: the bylaws outline the powers of the board in terms of what actions they can/cannot perform
- The number directors that can serve on the board at any given time
- The number of terms any individual board member can serve
- How to create new positions on the board
- How to fill board vacancies due to death, resignation, removal or term expiration of a board member
- How to resign from the board
- How to remove a member of the board
- Meetings

- Notice of meetings (notice requirements/waiver of notice)
- Place of Meetings
- Rules for special meetings (any meeting that is called outside of the annual meeting(s)
- Telephone meetings
- Adjournment of meetings (a meeting cannot end unless or until it is officially adjourned)
- Quorum (presence of a majority of all members required in order for a vote to be taken at a meeting)

- Order of command (for example, who will act in an officer's stead if absent or the position is vacant)
- What actions, if any, can be taken without a meeting.
- The creation and dissolution of board of directors' committees and subcommittees

Officers

Elected by the corporation's board of directors,

corporation officers are employees and agents of the corporation and include high-level executives such as the President, Vice President, Treasurer and Corporate Secretary. Some companies use titles like Chief Executive Officer (CEO), Chief Operating Officer (COO), or Chief Financial Officer (CFO) to describe their officers. Both styles of titling are acceptable. However, some state statutes require a corporation to have a President, Treasurer, Secretary and/or Vice President (Vice Presidents are sometimes optional). In those states, the CEOs of companies are often titled, "President and CEO." Be sure to check with your state's laws to determine what officers you are required to elect for your business.

The role of the officers is to manage the day-to-day operations of the corporation, subject to the direction and control of the board. Generally, the board will set forth the specific roles, powers and responsibilities of the officers in the corporation's bylaws. The bylaws, not any state or federal laws, control and establish acceptable actions of the officers.

Stock Issuance

Stocks are units (also referred to as shares) of

ownership that are sold as a means to raise capital for a corporation. The owners of stocks are the company's shareholders (also referred to as stockholders). The stock provision of a corporation's bylaws should set forth the number of shares that a corporation will issue, the classes of stock that will be issued and the receipts or stock certificates that shall be issued to stockholders to memorialize the sale of a share of stock. This provision also sets forth how stock certificates will be drafted and how records of stock certificates will be maintained. Maintaining proper records of stock certificates is extremely important. A company must be able to easily identify all stockholders as well as the number of stock currently issued and outstanding. Failure to do so could mean big trouble for a corporation if an auditor comes calling.

This provision should also set forth the process through which stock can be sold or transferred. While the actual creation and issuance of stock can be fairly complicated, the stock issuance section of a corporation's bylaws is generally short and to the point.

Because there are so many things that need to be ironed out in the bylaws as it pertains to the issuance/classification of stock, the board may execute a separate agreement called a shareholders' agreement to specifically address the agreement amongst the shareholders. If the board elects to draft a separate document, then the board should reference the stockholder agreement or its intent to create one in the stock issuance section of the bylaws.

*Please Note: this provision does not apply to nonprofit corporations.

Section 4.3 Partnership Agreements

Partnership Agreements are very much like Operating Agreements. The chief difference is that operating agreements are used to govern limited liability companies and partnership agreements are used to govern partnerships. Otherwise, the provisions and arrangements tend to look very much alike, with one exception. Because partnerships provide no limited liability for owners like LLCs and corporations, partnership agreements MUST specify how liability will be allocated amongst the partners through carefully crafted liability, insurance and indemnity provisions. Operating agreements and bylaws also have indemnity provisions, but again without the protection of limited liability, these provisions are even more important in partnership agreements.

For guidance on how to structure partnership agreements, refer to <u>Section 4.1</u> on operating agreements. For more information about indemnity clauses and how they fit into an agreement, refer to <u>Section 7.2</u> on interpreting basic contracts.

STEP 5

GET A WEBSITE:

PRIVACY POLICIES AND TERMS & CONDITIONS

If you're going to have a business, you MUST have a website. PERIOD! This is not negotiable. Your website is your calling card. Think about it. When someone recommends a new restaurant, clothing store, dog groomer… whatever. What is the first thing you do? Well, the first thing you do is go to YELP® to find some reviews. But, the second thing you do is go to their website! It may take some time before you're getting your own rave reviews on YELP®, but you can certainly have a strong digital presence through your website as soon as you get started.

To make sure that your business is just as protected "in the cloud" as it is on the ground, you will need a privacy policy and standard terms and conditions. Privacy policies and website terms and conditions act as warning labels for your website, products and/or services. They set expectations and provide general information to your users about what will happen as a result of: 1) sharing personal information with you, 2) buying your products and/or   3) using your service(s).

Unfortunately, most of your website users will never read either your privacy policy or terms and conditions. But alas, as with any good disclaimer, you throw it out there not because you think someone will actually read it. You put it on there because in the event that things go awry, you can point to your disclaimer, look a person square in the eye and say, "I told you so."

Section 5.1 Privacy Policies
What is it?

A privacy policy is a legal document or notice that discloses a website owner's practices for collecting, using, maintaining, protecting and/or disclosing the information it gathers through its website from website visitors, users and customers.

Why do you need one?

In this day and age, information is just as, if not more, useful than cash. It can be sold for money and other valuable consideration. It can be used as leverage or ransom against the companies, government entities or individuals who store it. Mismanagement of it can even cost you a presidential election (sorry Hilary). Accordingly, as a website owner (which you undoubtedly will be at some point during your entrepreneurial journey), it is important to have a legal mechanism, in the form of a privacy policy, that not only informs your website users of what you do with their private information but also provides you some protection in the event their information ends up in the wrong hands.

Another good reason to have a privacy policy is that it is legally required by several federal statutes and most state statutes. The state where you operate may not have laws (yet) that require website owners to have privacy policies. However, your website will reach users all over the world. In the event that your website is visited by a person in a state with robust privacy laws like California or Massachusetts, it is better to be safe than sorry and have your policy in place as soon as your website goes live.

There are also several third-party vendors (third party vendors include various plug-ins or apps like Adsense®, Google® analytics or Amazon® affiliates) that require website owners to have privacy policies in place as a prerequisite to using their service. Make sure to check a third-party vendor's standard terms and conditions prior to using their service to ensure that your privacy policy is in compliance with their privacy policy requirements.

Who needs it?

Any website that collects "private" information needs a privacy policy. So how "private" does the information have to be for your company to be subject to privacy policy laws? As it turns out, not that private.
If your website collects any of the following kinds of information:

- Names
- Mailing addresses
- Shipping addresses

- Dates of birth
- Phone numbers
- Credit card information (does not apply if payments are processed through third party websites like PayPal, Stripe or Square)
- Social security numbers
- Fax numbers

Through various information collection techniques such as:

- Comment forms
- Contact forms
- Cookies that remember names and/or email addresses
- Sign-ups for email lists
- Website registrations for "log-in only" users
- Google analytics tracking
- Facebook page plug-ins
- User tracking plug-ins
- Advertising programs

YOU NEED A PRIVACY POLICY.

What should be in it?

What should be in your privacy policy will vary depending on a number of things including but not limited to: (a) the type of business you promote on your website (e-commerce, financial institution, fashion blog etc.); (b) the kind of information you collect (names, email addresses, birth dates etc.); and (c) what you plan to do with the information. The following is a general overview of things to consider for your privacy policy, but you may need to make additional considerations for your individual policy depending on your business needs.

- The name, location and contact information for the person or business entity that owns and operates the website (so that users can contact you if they have further questions).
- The exact URL of your website
- Details regarding the kind of information you're collecting
- Why you are collecting the information
- How you're collecting the information (you may be collecting it in several ways like a member login registration, mailing list sign-up, "Contact Us" form, Google Analytics etc.)
- Who (if anyone) you plan to share personal information with
- How users can block cookies and opt out of third party advertisements
- Any third-party services/advertisers you're using to collect, process and/or store personal information
- How you plan to protect and store user information
- The effective date of the policy
- How updates to the policy will be posted on the website and communicated to users

Where should it be displayed?

Your privacy policy should be prominent and easy to find. Most website operators include their privacy policies on the footers of their websites. This way the policy is accessible from every page of the site but does not take up a significant amount of room on any particular page.

 Just So You Know:

If you're in need of a privacy policy and don't want to pay for one, check out your website provider's "help" page. That page should provide some guidance on privacy policies and how to craft them. Your website provider may even have a sample policy that you can use. Wordpress, for example, has a great Privacy Policy Help Page that includes a sample privacy policy.

You can also look at the privacy policies of bigger, more established businesses that provide similar products and/or services as your business, for guidance on how to craft your own policy. Their policies were most likely drafted by a team of lawyers who, undoubtedly, already took into consideration the same things that you should take into consideration when drafting your policy. #youreWELCOME

Section 5.2 Website Terms and Conditions

What is it?

Website terms and conditions (also referred to as terms of use) constitute a binding legal agreement between a website and its users that sets forth the rules/regulations for use of the website and the products and/or services offered by the website.

Who needs it?

Everyone who owns and operates a website.

Why do you need it?

The use of website terms and conditions is not required by law. However, as a new business owner, it is important to limit your potential liability to as many parties as possible including: customers, vendors, business partners, employees, AND website users. Placing a terms and conditions page on your website will provide you with some protection from being sued by your website users.

How do you make them enforceable?

Clickwrap vs. Browser Terms of Use Agreements

"Wait, I never signed a terms and conditions agreement!" "How can you prove that I agreed to it?" Those are the first words website users will proclaim if ever forced to abide by a website's terms and conditions. However, in the age of technology, you don't necessarily have to physically sign a contract to be bound by its terms.

If website users don't have to sign your terms and conditions page to be forced to abide by them, how can you craft your website's terms and conditions in a way that makes them binding on all who visit your website? This section will provide some insight into the different kinds of website terms and conditions, and how to implement them in a way that maximizes their effectiveness.

Clickwrap Terms of Use Agreements

There are two kinds of website terms and conditions agreements: Clickwrap and Browser. Clickwrap (or clickthrough) terms of use agreements are website terms and conditions that are presented to users prior to website entry and requires them to click an "I accept" or "I agree" button before being granted permission to use the site. If the user does not click the "I accept" or "I agree" button, then he/she will not be allowed to enter the website or use the service/product. You often see this kind of terms and conditions agreement used by larger companies like Apple®, Google® or Yahoo® or higher risk companies like social media platforms and sites that sell products (e-commerce) directly to consumers from their site.

This is attributed to the fact that Clickwrap terms of use agreements provide website owners with the greatest legal protections. Requiring website users to affirmatively accept terms and conditions by clicking an "I agree" button, has the same force and effect of having them sign a contract. Larger companies need this extra protection to limit their potential of being sued by the millions of people who visit their websites daily. They also do it….well, because they can. Larger companies (1) know that most people won't be deterred from using their service by having to click an extra button; and (2) most people won't read them anyway.

Think about it. Has having to click the "I agree" button to the Apple® terms and conditions on your iPhone® ever stopped you from getting the latest IOS update? Absolutely not. However, by clicking that button, you have essentially bound yourself to WHATEVER rules and regulations Apple® has regarding the use of its software, even if those terms are against your best interest. Why do you click? Because you love Apple® and you want your update. You also "know" Apple®. You trust Apple®. You have been using Apple® since you got your first phone in eighth grade. Apple® would never hurt you, right? This is definitely not true, but the size of the brand offers you some comfort in potentially signing your life and rights away.

This type of terms and conditions agreement is generally not as effective for smaller brands. There is considerably less trust in a brand that is not as established. Thus, requiring users to agree to your terms and conditions prior to admission to your site may deter potential users and customers from visiting. Think about it. If you visited susansweaters.com and it asked you to agree to a 40-page terms of use agreement prior to entry to the site, would you click "I agree?" No!! You would just go to sarahssweaters.com and get your sweaters there.

However, if you are a high-risk or large company and you decide that Clickwrap terms of use agreements make the most sense for your business, here are some tips for "beefing up" the likelihood of enforceability of your Clickwrap terms of use agreement:

1. Include a clearly visible statement next to the "I Agree" button saying that "the user has read and agrees to the terms."

2. Do not preselect the "I Agree" button. Require the user to affirmatively select the "I Agree" button.

3. Place the "I Agree" button at the end of the terms and conditions page so that the user has to physically scroll through the terms and conditions to get to the "I Agree" button.

Browser Terms of Use Agreements

Legally protecting your business is a constant balancing act between doing what's best for you and what's best for business. As a new business-owner, unless you have the next Uber® on your hands, what's best for business is probably a Browser terms of use agreement. Browser terms of use agreements are website terms and conditions that are made available to users through links on the website but do not require visitors to take any affirmative action indicating agreement to the terms. The terms instead state that use of the site is deemed to be acceptance of the terms. Because users don't have to demonstrate acceptance of the terms by signing or clicking an "I agree" button, these types of terms and conditions generally provide less protection than Clickwrap terms of use agreements. While Browser terms of use agreements provide less protection, they do provide some protection making them worthwhile investments for your website. You also don't have the goodwill or brand recognition of an Apple® or Google® (yet), so you don't want to risk losing customers over your terms and conditions by implanting a Clickwrap terms of use agreement.

If you determine that a Browser terms of use agreement is most appropriate for your business, here are some things that you can do to increase the enforceability of your Browser terms of use agreement:

1. The first argument website users will make to get around the enforceability of Browser terms of use agreements is that they didn't know about it or didn't see it. To avoid this, try placing your Terms of Use button in the header or menu of your homepage, instead of

or in addition to, the footer. Putting it in a prominent place will reduce the chances of someone saying they didn't know about or see your terms of use.

2. In the body of the policy, be sure to include language like, "use of this page constitutes acceptance of these terms and conditions." In order for a contract to be enforceable, there must be evidence that both parties agree to its terms. Including this kind of language will provide some method of acceptance for the other party outside of clicking or signing something to evidence agreement.

3. Provide a notice stating that, "the website is governed by the terms of use and that use of the site constitutes acceptance of the terms. This is an added layer of protection in case website users don't actually read your terms and conditions. The best place to put this button is right next to your terms and conditions link or button. However, I understand if you don't want to clutter up

your header with this notice, but at least include it in your footer.

Just So You Know:

When drafting or selecting terms and conditions and privacy policies for your website, make sure they are:

(1) easy to read and understand by your users;

(2) free of any spelling or grammatical errors;

(3) consistent with each other as well as, client agreements, notices, third party vendor agreements, disclaimers and statements; and

(4) reviewed and regularly updated to reflect any changes in legal requirements, new products and/or services or other changes to the site.

STEP 6

GET PROTECTED:

INTELLECTUAL PROPERTY AND LICENSING

Together, copyrights, trademarks and patents comprise an area of law known as intellectual property. Intellectual property is a type of property that includes intangible creations of the mind like ideas, designs and art. As society has progressed towards an economy grounded in intangible ideas vs. tangible assets, intellectual property has become increasingly important to the strength of businesses, especially new ones. There's nothing worse than seeing the logo, idea, words, invention etc., that you labored so intensely over stolen by someone else (please insert Melania Trump's 2017 United Nations speech here). Especially if that someone else is making millions at your expense. To protect your intellectual property from infringement, you will need to obtain a copyright, trademark or patent, or some combination of the three depending on your business. This chapter will explain the purpose of copyrights, trademarks and patents, and how you can use them to protect your business.

Section 6.1 Copyrights

What is it?

A copyright is an intellectual property protection that grants authors or owners of creative works the exclusive right to publish, use, distribute, sell, license, perform, display, reproduce and recreate said works. Per U.S. Copyright law, a creative work is "an original work of authorship fixed in any tangible medium of expression, now known or later developed, from which they can be perceived, reproduced, or otherwise communicated, either directly or with the aid of a machine or device." What you need to know from that formal definition of copyright is that to be eligible for copyright protection you MUST be

(1) the author(s)/creator(s)/owner of; (2) an ORIGINAL (3) WORK that is (4) FIXED in a tangible medium of expression. Let's dig a little deeper and explore all four requirements of copyright eligibility to help you determine what is necessary to qualify for copyright protection.

(1) Copyright Ownership

The general rule of law for copyright ownership is as follows: whoever creates the work owns it. You don't have to file a copyright application, register your work or idea…nothing. If you created the work, then you are the author/owner, PERIOD. This is good news for creators and authors. But as a business owner, you may have logos, works of art, blog posts, books, jingles, photos, graphics etc. that you have others create for your business that you want ownership of. How do you go about obtaining ownership of creative works developed for your business that you did not create? The following list illustrates several ways that you can obtain ownership of your logo, photos, graphics, jingles etc.:

- **Create the work yourself.** Obviously, the easiest way to own your work is to CREATE IT! Because copyright ownership/protection automatically vests in the creator of the work; if you create your work, you own it! BUT if the work you are seeking to protect is also a logo, consider seeking trademark protection in lieu of copyright protection. I will explain why in Section 6.2 on trademarks.

- **Create part of the work**. A joint work is a work prepared by two or more individuals with the intention that their separate contributions be merged into a single work. Authors own the work jointly and equally, unless the authors make an agreement stating otherwise. Each joint author has the right to exercise any or all of the exclusive rights granted to all copyright owners including but not limited to: licensing the work, transferring his or her entire ownership interest to another person without the other joint authors' consent and update the work for his or her own purpose. If you don't wish to own the work equally, you can use a statement of joint work to outline the following: each individual author's ownership interest in the work, each author's share of any revenues generated by exploitation of the mark, marketing rights, use rights and infringement prosecution rights.

- **Copyright assignment agreement**. A copyright assignment agreement is an instrument/document that transfers ownership of a copyright from one party to another. This type of agreement is ideal for "one-off" or isolated situations when you contract an artist, designer, photographer or musician etc. for their services. You may have to pay the other party in exchange for ownership rights of the work. But once the agreement is executed, (both parties sign it) the work will be all yours.

- **Work for hire clause/agreement**. A work made for hire is a work that is created by an employee or independent contractor for an employer. If you hire someone to perform work for you on a regular or consistent basis, make sure you include a work for hire provision in your independent contractor or employment agreement. The provision will stipulate that any work created by the employee/independent contractor during the course of his/her employment shall be automatically owned by the employer (you). You however, may not have any ownership rights to the work the employee/independent contractor creates on his/her own time with his/her own money, equipment and/or resources.

(2) Copyright Originality

In an age where nothing is new or novel and just about everything has been done before, is anything really original? How "original" does your work have to be to be eligible for copyright protection? Luckily for you, not that original! Copyright law states that "original" means (1) not copied and (2) at least minimally creative. Minimal creativity sets the bar for the requisite level of creativity extremely low. Even a small amount of creativity will suffice. The law states that "a work may be original even though it closely resembles other works so long as the similarity is fortuitous (coincidence) and not the result of copying. For example, assume that two poets, each ignorant of the other, compose identical poems. Neither work is novel, yet both are original [because neither copied the other] and hence, copyrightable."

(3) Copyrightable Works

Copyright law lists eight kinds of creative works that are protected under copyright law. That list includes:

- literary works (books, articles, poems, plays, screen writings etc.);
- musical works (including any accompanying words);
- dramatic works (including any accompanying music);
- pantomimes and choreographic works (dance);
- pictorial, graphic, and sculptural works (photos, paintings, memes, clip art, statues etc.);
- motion pictures and other audiovisual works (movies, television shows, cartoons, gifs etc.);
- sound recordings (noises, recorded sounds, recorded speeches etc.); and
- architectural works (buildings, blue prints, structures etc.).

However, while this list is illustrative, it is not exhaustive. Due to the ever-changing landscape of creative works and constantly evolving technologies, the list of works protected by copyright law is long and constantly in-flux.

(4) Fixed in a Tangible Medium

Fixed in a tangible medium means that the idea must exist in some physical or visual format outside of your mind. This means that mere ideas do not count and cannot be protected by copyright law. You must have actually created the song, painting, poem etc. in order for it to be eligible for copyright protection. Accordingly, be careful with whom you share ideas with. Until your work exists in some physical form, there is no way to protect it.

Why do you need it?

You do not have to file a copyright application to receive copyright protections. Some level of copyright protection exists for authors who meet the four requirements of copyright eligibility (as discussed above) as soon as it becomes fixed in a tangible medium. However, copyright registration is required to establish a case of copyright infringement and sue a potential infringer for statutory damages (statutory damages for infringement range from \$75 to \$150,000 per work infringed). This means you cannot stop others from copying and using your work without first filing a copyright application. Further, copyright registration establishes a timeline for when the work was created and provides potential infringers with notice that you created the work first.

How long will protection last?

Once registered, copyright protection lasts for the life of the author plus seventy (70) years from the time of death.

How do you register a work for copyright protection?

In order to file a copyright, you must submit the following to the U.S. Copyright Office:

(1) a copyright application form which is a basic form that asks for general information like the name of

the work, a description of the work and the owner of the work;

(2) a copy of the work being filed; and

(3) a filing fee (ranging from $35-$55 depending on the kind of application filed).

 Just So You Know:

Unless filing a joint work (work with more than one author), or many works at the same time, filing a copyright application is fairly quick and easy. You should have no problem filing an application on your own. The U.S. Copyright Office offers an online filing option. For works that can be transmitted digitally, you can complete the entire process online. For works that cannot be transmitted digitally, you can file your application online and mail your physical work separately.

Section 6.2 Trademarks

What is it?

Trademark law encompasses both trademarks (symbols, words, logos, slogans etc. associated with *goods*) and service marks (symbols, words, logos, slogans etc. associated with *services*) and focuses on the protection of symbols, words, phrases and names which identify the source of goods and/or services associated with those goods and/or services. The basic policy behind trademark law is to protect goodwill developed in connection with a particular mark which has been adopted and used by an entity to identify it as the source of those goods and/or service.

Simply put, trademarks help consumers identify what's "on the inside of the packaging" based on what's displayed on the outside. For example, if you go to the grocery store and pick up a box of Lucky Charms®, you know exactly what you will find on the inside of that box. You know exactly how it will taste, what it will look like and how it will smell because you know what the red box with the leprechaun on the front that reads "Lucky Charms®" represents. Further, it doesn't matter how many Sporty Charms, Thrifty Charms or Golden Charms are on the shelf, because while similar to Lucky Charms®, they are not similar enough that you would mistake them for the original.

Let's apply this same idea to slogans. If I say, "Just do it." You automatically think Nike®. If I say, "Melts in your mouth, not in your hands." You automatically think M&M's®. Why? Because trademark laws prevent any other athletic apparel, equipment, shoe company etc., from using the words "Just do it" in connection with their goods!! I don't even have to say the word Nike, but you know that "Just do it" IS Nike®. That, ladies and gentlemen, is the power of branding and the power of trademarks. This is why knowing, understanding and having a trademark is crucial to the creation and protection of both your business and brand.

What kind of marks are granted protection?

The standards for trademark protection are considerably greater than they are for copyright protection. You cannot slap any old mark on your good or service and expect the United States Patent and Trademark Office (USPTO) to protect it. The USPTO considers several factors when determining whether to grant your mark with trademark protection. The three most significant factors are (1) whether or not your mark is *confusingly similar* to a mark that has already been registered; (2) the *strength of your mark* and (3) whether or not you are *using the mark in commerce*.

(1) Confusingly Similar Marks

Obviously, if someone is already using the mark

you want to register AND has already registered said mark with the USPTO, then NO you cannot register that mark with the USPTO. Further, if you use that mark, you may also run the risk of getting hit with a cease and desist letter from the registered owner of the mark, sooooooo WATCH YOURSELF.

What may not be quite as obvious is that you also may not use your mark if it is CONFUSINGLY similar to a mark that has already been registered. The test for confusingly similar marks is not concrete, but U.S. courts have identified seven factors crucial to making a determination of confusing similarity between marks. The seven factors that the courts (and you should) consider are as follows:

   a. **Relatedness of Goods or Services** - The USPTO has identified 45 classes that goods and services can fall into, the first 34 classes are for goods and the last 11 classes are for services. In order to file a trademark, you must identify the class of goods/services you wish to file your trademark under. Some classes are closely related like shoes and apparel and some are completely unrelated like textiles and bridges. The USPTO will allow for similar marks to be registered so long as they are not filed in the same or similar class. For example, you can file a trademark for "Bubba" Champagne and someone else might also be allowed to register a trademark for "Bubba" Cars. Why? Because it's highly unlikely that anyone would confuse your Bubba Champagne for Bubba Cars. The less related the goods, the more likely you will be granted trademark protection even for marks that are very similar.

b. **Similarity of Marks** – Marks don't have to be identical to be deemed similar. But how close is too close? The test used for similarity can be quite subjective and hard to characterize. So, rather than try to explain, I will just show you some marks deemed too similar for registration by U.S. courts.

Confusingly Similar Marks	
MAGNAVOX	MULTIVOX
SIMONIZ	PERMANIZE
PLATINUM PUFF	PLATINUM PLUS
ZIRCO	COZIRC
MATERNALLY YOURS	YOUR MATERNITY SHOP

c. **Similarity in Appearance** - If a mark that looks the same as yours, even if not the same, is already registered, you still may not be allowed to register your mark. Some examples are as follows:

Marks Similar in Appearance	
LUTEX	LUTEXAL
NEWPORT	NEWPORTS
MILTRONICS	MILTRON
TURCOOL	TRUCOOL

d. **Similarity in Sound -** You also may not be allowed to register your mark if there is a registered mark that is not the same as yours but sounds the same when read aloud.

Marks that Sound the Same	
CRESCO	KRESSCO
SEYCOS	SEIKO
CANYA	CANA
ENTELEC	INTELECT

e. **Similarity in Meaning -** You must also be careful of marks that are not the same but mean the same thing, especially if filed in the same class. For example, "Pledge Cards" and "Promise Cards" are too similar in meaning to be filed in the same class because pledge and promise mean almost the same thing.

f. **Design Marks -** Not all trademarks are words. Some trademarks consist of pictures or logos also known as design marks. You also will not be allowed to register a logo or picture that is similar to one already registered.

g. **Likely to Deceive -** You will not be allowed to register a mark if you selected it solely with the intention to deceive the general public.

The whole purpose of trademarks is to prevent others from benefiting from the goodwill of another's brand. Accordingly, it would not be fair to allow someone to file a trademark for "Tiphany's" hoping the general public might mistake it for "Tiffany's."

When trying to determine of whether or not your mark is confusingly similar to one that is already registered, consider all of the above factors, not just one or two or even three. Your mark must not be confusingly similar to another, already registered mark, on any of the above fronts to be granted trademark protection.

(2) Strength of the Mark

The USPTO assesses the strength of a trademark based on a spectrum of protectability ranging from arbitrary to generic. The strongest marks are fanciful or arbitrary and granted the most protection. Suggestive and/or descriptive marks fall in the middle of the spectrum and are granted some protection. While generic marks are at the opposite end of the spectrum and are considered the weakest kind of mark, meaning they are not granted any trademark protection.

STRONG MARKS: A strong mark is a mark that is fanciful or arbitrary. That means the mark is entirely unrelated to your product or service. Consider this: What does a Puma have to do with athletic gear? What does Uber have to do with public transportation?? ABSOLUTELY NOTHING!!! The only reason we associate Puma with athletic gear is because Puma told us we should by selling athletic gear with Puma written on it. The arbitrariness of their mark makes it STRONG. Because you wouldn't normally associate Pumas with athletic gear, Puma is allowed to protect its brand by having the ability to stop others from slapping Puma on a sneaker and calling it their own.

WEAK MARKS: A weak mark is one that is descriptive or generic. This means your mark describes the nature of your product/service or it is a word commonly used in connection with your product/service. Consider this. If you make sandals and you want to call your company "SANDALS," is it fair to prevent EVERY other shoe/sandal company from using the word sandal?

ABSOLUTELY NOT! Try coming up with a name that people wouldn't normally associate with sandals. You will be more likely to gain trademark protection for your mark if you do.

(3) Use of the Mark in Commerce

When filing a trademark application, you must provide a basis for filing. The USPTO provides two bases for filing: (1) use of the mark in commerce and (2) *intent* to use the mark in commerce. "In commerce" means selling your goods or services in connection with your trademark and making a showing that people associate your mark with the sale of your goods and/or services.

However, if you haven't started using your mark in commerce yet, but want to reserve your mark to keep potential infringers at bay while gearing up for your big launch, you have two options:

Option 1: Take a chance and wait until you begin using the mark in connection with the sale of your product, service or good before filing your trademark application.

Option 2: File an "Intent to Use" application with the USPTO. The USPTO will allow you to file an "intent to use" trademark application as long as you ACTUALLY use (not think about using, considering using or 'bout to, maybe, kinda use but actually USE) the mark within six (6) months of approval of your "intent to use" application. If you are ready to file your mark within the six-month period, you will have to submit a statement of use and pay an additional fee to officially register your mark. If you need more than six (6) months, you can file a request for an extension.

Why do you need it?

Trademark registration is not required in order to receive basic trademark protection. You receive some trademark protection (common law trademark) just from USING your mark in connection with the sale of your good, service or product. Once you start using your mark, you can use the ™ symbol regardless of whether or not you have filed a trademark application with the USPTO. However, using the symbol may not work to your benefit. It will alert others to the fact that you have not registered your mark with the USPTO and thus have no power to pursue any infringement actions against potentially infringing parties.

So, in answer to the original question: why do you need it? You need to register your trademark because you MUST have a registered trademark with the USPTO in order to establish a case of trademark infringement. Trademark registration gives you the legal "teeth" that you need in order to protect your mark. After all, what is the point of having a cool trademark and establishing a killer brand if you cannot stop others from stealing it from you? Not to mention, you get to put this ® next to your logo. Also consider this: What if someone else registers your mark first and later tries to sue you for infringement or stop you from using it? Would be a bad day for business, wouldn't it?

How long will protection last?

Trademark protection lasts as long as you use the mark in commerce. As long as you use it, you won't lose it. However, you will need to renew your trademark application after five years of use and again after ten years of use. After your tenth year, you will need to submit renewal applications every ten years.

How do you register one?

The trademark registration process is a tad more complicated than the copyright application process. The following is an outline of the registration process:

Step 1: Search. Conducting a search is not required to file a trademark. However, performing a thorough search of previously filed marks is important to assess the strength of your mark. There is no point in filing an application for a mark that's already registered. Plus, the USPTO will not give you a refund if you do.

Step 2: File an application. File an application and submit a fee to the USPTO. There are several kinds of applications you can file, all with their own fee structures. Be sure you know which application is appropriate for your mark prior to filing.

Step 3: Wait forever. It generally takes 4-5 months before the USPTO will assign an examining attorney to your case. So, once you file, chill for a bit.

Step 4: Respond to Objections. Examining attorneys will review your application to determine whether or not it meets the criteria for trademark protection. If your application passes muster, then you will glide to step five. If it does not, the examining attorney will object to approval of your application through an "office action." Office actions can vary in severity from objections to a misspelled word to allegations that your mark is confusingly similar to an already registered mark. Responses to office actions can be difficult to navigate alone. If you get one, it may be a good time to call an attorney.

Step 5: Publication. Once you make it through the "Office Action Gauntlet," your mark will be published for opposition. This will give the general public an opportunity to object to your mark if they believe it may infringe upon another mark. If an opposition is filed, the matter will go before the Trademark Trial and Appeal Board to be resolved. This is very similar to a court proceeding... and an even better time to call an attorney.

Step 6: Registration! If your application is unopposed or you successfully overcome opposition, you will be issued a certificate of registration.

From beginning to end, the trademark registration process can take anywhere from 8 months (in a perfect world) to 18 months (an average world) and beyond (the real world). However, if granted registration, trademark protection will commence from the date of filing.

Section 6.3 Patents

What is it?

Ok, so for a quick recap: copyrights protect ideas and trademarks/service marks protect brands. Patents protect inventions. A patent is an exclusive right to exclude others from making, using, selling, licensing, importing or otherwise profiting from your invention. If your business involves the sale of a "new and useful" product, formula, design, process, composition of matter or any new and useful improvement of an already discovered product, formula, design etc., you need a patent.

What kinds of things can be patented?

In order to be granted patent protection, your invention must be new, useful and non-obvious.

    (a) New or Novel. Patent law has defined new as something that: "(1) has not previously been patented, described in a printed publication, or in public use, on sale, or otherwise available to the public before the effective filing date of the claimed invention or (2) was described in a patent issued by the U.S. or in an application for patent published or deemed by the U.S., in which the patent or application, as the case may be, names another inventor and was effectively filed before the effective filing date of the claimed invention." In short, if it's been patented before, then it ain't new. Further, if your invention is an improvement upon a prior invention, it must involve at least one difference from the prior art to be considered new or novel.

    (b) Usefulness. Inventions that are "useful" are ones that have a useful purpose and are operative. This means that the machine or product MUST operate to perform the intended purpose in order to be considered useful and thus worthy of patent protection.

(c) Non-Obviousness. For an invention to be non-obvious, it must be sufficiently different from what has been described in any version of the inventions before it. Your improvement to the prior invention also must not be obvious to a person having ordinary skill in the area related to the invention. For example, changing the color or size of a prior invention will not get you a patent.

What kinds of patents are there?

There are two major categories of patents: utility and design. There is a third category of patent: the plant patent. However, it is such a specialized area of patents, that unless you're a botanist with a PhD in agriculture and forestry, it likely won't apply to you. Thus, we won't be discussing it here. Instead, we will focus on the more common categories of patents: design and utility.

Design Patents

A design patent protects the ornamental or

aesthetic design of an article of manufacture. Simply put, a design patent covers the way an invention looks. It does not cover the article itself, the way it functions or any internal mechanical structure. Design patents cover things like packaging, colors and texture. They generally consist of drawings that show the invention from six angles: top, bottom, front, back, left and right.

Obtaining a design patent is relatively easy compared to obtaining a utility patent and is considerably less expensive. But design patents are considered weaker forms of protection because design patents only protect the way a thing looks.

How long will the protection last?
The term of a design patent is 15 years measured from the date of grant.

How do I get a design patent?
The registration process for a design patent is fairly similar to filing an application for a trademark.

Step 1: Conduct a search. How can you determine if your design is new if you don't know what other designs are out there? Be sure to search for previously registered patents prior to submitting your application.

Step 2: File an application. File an application and submit a fee to the USPTO. In addition to the application filing fee, a search fee and examination fee are also required. However, if the applicant is a small entity, (an independent inventor, small business or nonprofit organization), these fees may be reduced by half.

Step 3: **Examination.** Your application will be assigned to an examining attorney who will review the merits of your application.

Step 4: Respond to Objections. If a patent-examining attorney objects to your application, they will submit an office action. You can respond to the office action or withdraw your application and try to file a new one. If you respond to the office action and successfully defend your application, the examining attorney will rescind his/her office action. If you are not successful, your application will be rejected.

Step 5: Registration. If you successfully make it through the examination process and any outstanding office actions, your application will be approved.

Utility Patents
What is it?

A utility patent is granted to anyone who invents or discovers any new and useful process, machine, article of manufacture, or composition of matter, or any new and useful improvement thereof. A utility patent focuses on the functionality of an invention and whether or not it actually does what you intend it to.

How long will the protection last?

The term of a utility patent is 20 years from the date the application for the patent is filed in the United States. U.S. patent grants are effective only within the United States, U.S. territories and U.S. possessions. Under certain circumstances, patent term extensions or adjustments may be available.

How do you get one?

To obtain a utility patent, you will need to submit an application and the appropriate fees to the USPTO.

However, the requisite application for utility patents is quite long and can be rather difficult to navigate alone. As a result, if you need a utility patent, then I would say that you also NEED an attorney. Obtaining a utility patent is a very difficult, delicate and intricate process. I would not recommend navigating this process alone. However, if you cannot afford to hire an attorney, the USPTO has an excellent Pro Se Assistance Program designed to aid inventors navigate the patent application process without the aid of an attorney.

 Just So You Know: Patent law is its own separate area of the law. Lawyers wishing to practice patent law must have a background in the sciences and pass a patent bar examination. The patent bar examination is a licensing exam for lawyers who wish to practice patent law. Accordingly, you will have to seek out a patent attorney, licensed to practice patent law to help you file your application. So please, do not ask Johnny the Ticket Lawyer to help you file your patent application.

Section 6.4 Intellectual Property Licensing

Just because you can't touch intellectual property, doesn't mean it isn't valuable. Just like any other kind of property, patents, trademarks and copyrights can also be leveraged in exchange for money. One of the most common ways to exploit intellectual property aside from selling it is to license it. A license is a right granted to another which gives him/her permission to do something which he or she could not legally do absent such permission. In the case of intellectual property, licensing means giving someone permission to use your creative work, trademark or invention in exchange for a licensing fee.

Now I'm sure you're asking yourself, "why would I want to give someone else permission to use my stuff?" My answer, "So you can make more MONEY." The following examples will help to illustrate how licenses work and why they can play an integral role in maximizing the profitability of your intellectual property.

Licensing Hypos

The first hypo illustrates how you might be able to use a license to exploit your patent.

Hypo #1

You are a technological genius who has a patent on a new widget that has the potential to change the world forever. However, you aren't a business person and don't want to put in the time, effort, energy or cash required to bring your widget to market. You also don't want to sell your patent and lose it forever. To retain the rights to your patent and bring your widget to the masses without having to do any of the heavy lifting, you can grant someone else who does have the time, effort, energy AND cash, a license to exploit (market, sell, develop...etc.) your patent in exchange for a fee. You will retain ownership of the patent, but they will have the right to use it for whatever length of time you allow them to for whatever purpose you specify. Awesome, right?

Now, let's apply this same principle to trademarks.

Hypo #2

You are the owner of a wildly successful dishware company called, "Delicate Dishes." You are a dish expert and know the dish business inside out. However, to capitalize on your popularity in the kitchenware space, you decide it's time to expand your business to include oven mitts. Unfortunately, you don't know anything about oven mitts. It's also not worth your time to try and become an expert in oven mitts because you need to keep your focus on managing the dishes.

So, instead of trying to create the oven mitt line on

your own, you enlist the help of your cousin, Lonnie, who just so happens to be an oven mitt manufacturer. You want to give Lonnie permission to use your logo on his mitts. Accordingly, you grant him a *license* to use your "Delicate Dishes" logo in exchange for a license fee. The license will give Lonnie permission to manufacture his mitts with your logo on them. This is important because to the general public it will appear as though you are making the oven mitts. When in fact, Lonnie is making the oven mitts for you, leaving you with plenty of time to manage "Delicate Dishes."

In this scenario, everyone wins! You will profit from the sale of the mitts without having to make them because you will receive your licensing fee from Lonnie. Lonnie will also benefit because he will be able to sell more mitts from the use of your logo. He will hopefully sell so many more mitts that it will be worth it for him to give you a share of the profits in the form of a license fee.

Licensing Agreements

Ok, so now you want to license everything from the dog to the trademark, and maybe, the kids on occasion, right? Unfortunately, I can't help with a kid license, but I can help you identify the appropriate tool for granting a license: a licensing agreement. A licensing agreement is a legal document giving someone permission to use your marks in exchange for a fee or other valuable consideration. The following are some things that you should consider when drafting, reviewing or executing licensing agreements to exploit your intellectual property.

 Just So You Know:

> I will use the terms licensor and licensee frequently to describe the parties to a licensing agreement. The licensor is a person who owns the intellectual property and is granting the license. The licensee is the party who is licensing or being granted permission to use the intellectual property.

Important Licensing Agreement Provisions

- **Territory - T**erritory refers to the geographic scope of the license. For example, you can restrict a licensee's use of your mark to a specific region, city, state or country.

- **Term-** The term refers to the length of time both parties wish to be bound by the terms of the contract. Be careful of selecting a term that is too long. You don't want to lock yourself into a deal forever.

- **Purpose/Products -** It is extremely important to narrow the purpose of the license. Let's say you hire a marketing company to help promote your business. You will want to specify the purpose of the license to limit how, where and when they can use your intellectual property. If you don't limit the scope of the license, you may wake up and find your marketing company using your logo to promote its own business or services.

- **Exclusivity -** You can grant a licensee the exclusive right to license your property or you can grant them a non-exclusive right. Exclusive means that during the term of your agreement, the licensee will be the only one allowed to use your mark. You can also use other provisions like the purpose and territory to limit the scope of a licensee's exclusivity. For example, you may decide to grant the licensee the exclusive right to use your logo ONLY on *widgets* in *California*.

- **Quality Control -** Whenever you grant a licensee the right to use your intellectual property, you need to protect your brand by setting quality standards. For example, if you allow a licensee to use your trademark to sell their notebooks, you want to ensure that they are making quality notebooks. You also want to make sure that they are displaying your marks in the highest of resolutions with amazing clarity, consistent with how you display your marks in other places.

- **Approval Rights -** You can demand the right to approve the use of any of your intellectual property prior to use by a licensee. You should be reasonable with your approval rights by not withholding approval for frivolous reasons. However, if you believe that a licensee's suggested use of your mark is inconsistent with your brand, you can and should exercise your right to approve/reject the licensee's suggested use of the mark.

- **Definition of the Mark -** As a company, you may own several copyrights, trademarks or patents. To avoid any abuse or confusion, make sure you clearly define what intellectual property you are including in the agreement.

- **License Fees -** You can use several payment mechanisms to make money in a licensing deal. For example, you can require the licensor to pay a flat fee upfront for the use of the mark AND a royalty fee for continued use of the mark. A royalty is a percentage of the profits generated from the sale/use of the licensed material.

STEP 7

GET EDUCATED:

HOW TO INTERPRET A CONTRACT

There is absolutely no replacement for having access to a good attorney who can review and negotiate your contracts for you. However, as a fellow entrepreneur, I understand that you may not be able to afford to call your attorney to answer every question and review every agreement. To help you navigate, at minimum, the basic agreements that you will undoubtedly encounter as you start your business such as cell phone provider agreements, vendor agreements or office lease agreements, I have come up with five basic contract provisions that I believe every business owner, and quite frankly every person should know and understand. This chapter will also cover some other contract provisions that you should know called boilerplate provisions. Boilerplate provisions aren't as material to an agreement as the first five provisions discussed in this chapter. However, they can be found in just about every contract you'll ever read, making them really good things to know.

Section 7.1 Important Contract Provisions

To help provide you with an overview of the most important parts of a contract, I have compiled the following list. There are certainly other contract provisions that are important, but the following will give you a solid and BASIC understanding of what's important in a contract. Now you can save your pennies and only call your lawyer for the important stuff like trademark filings, contract drafting or policy creation. No need to say thank you, #yourewelcome.

Before getting started, I should also note that if you receive a contract that is missing any of these provisions, it's probably not a contract you want to sign. If you find yourself in a situation where the terms of your contract seem shaky, be sure to ask the opposing party and an attorney some additional questions before moving forward. Lastly, ye be warned. Reading this section will not give you every tool necessary to be a master of contracts. It will, however, give you just enough tools to be "contract dangerous." You will also have an idea of what you should be looking for and the types of questions you should be asking when reviewing various contracts, terms & conditions and agreements.

1. Parties.

A party to a contract is the person(s) or entity (company) meant to be bound by its terms. A good contract should clearly define who the parties are. Contracts generally do this by providing several identifying factors for each party including but not limited to:

- full name (applies to both individuals and businesses) including a DBA (doing business as) name,
- entity type (this can be a person, corporation, limited liability company, nonprofit corporation etc.),
- state of residence,
- address and/or

- telephone number.

The purpose of clearly defining the parties is to make it clear who is being bound. For example, if your name is John Smith, there are probably millions of John Smiths. The party identifiers should make it clear that the contract is referencing you vs. one of the million other John Smiths roaming the world.

2. Term

The term is the length of time that the contract is active or valid. The contract term should have a clear beginning and a clear end. The beginning is usually the date the contract is signed, but it may be another date if the contract states otherwise. The end date can also be given as a precise date, but that may not always be the case. Accordingly, you may find the end date stated as follows: "thirty days from the effective date." This means the contract will be active or valid for the 30 days immediately following the starting date.

When the end date is not stated as a specific day/time, make sure you are clear whether the contract will end "on" a certain date, "by" a certain date or "after" a certain date. Contract end dates that aren't specific can sometimes be tricky, but you can always include a specific end day/time to alleviate the possibility of any confusion. Regardless of the contract wording, it is important to make sure everyone is clear about when a contract begins and ends. No one wants to be bound forever!

3. Payment

Every contract MUST include a payment provision. For a contract to be valid there must be consideration (something of value) exchanged between the parties. This means that each party must receive something of value in exchange for what he/she is giving up. The "thing of value" does not have to be money. It can be some other form of property (tangible or otherwise) services, rights etc., that the parties deem to be of some value. Regardless of value, each party must give and receive something.

The contract should also include terms governing the nature of the payments such as:

- amount of payment(s),
- frequency of payment(s) (one time, weekly, monthly etc.), date of payment(s),
- forms of acceptable payment,

- places (bank account numbers, addresses, wiring instructions…etc.) where payments can be delivered,
- continued obligations to pay in the event of termination or expiration, and
- penalties for late or missed payments.

4. Termination

Contract termination is ending a contract prior to the date of expiration (the last day of the contract term). There are many reasons why you may need to end a contract early. Maybe you are no longer happy with your service(s)/good(s), or maybe you can no longer afford your service(s)/good(s). Make sure your contract states if and when you can terminate your contract as well as what steps you need to take to terminate the contract without breaching it. Many contracts require a penalty for terminating a contract early like a "termination" or "cancellation" fee. Whatever the penalties and/or steps are for termination (if any), make sure you are aware of them and make sure they are clearly stated.

5. Signature

For a contract to be valid, all parties must agree to its terms. The way that we show agreement is through signature. Make sure that all parties sign to ensure a contract's validity. Also note that: (1) if one of the parties is a minor, a parent or guardian may need to sign the contract as well (not all states require parental signature for all persons under the age of 18) and (2) if one or both parties are businesses, make sure that the person signing on behalf of the business has the authority to bind it.

Section 7.2 Boilerplate Contract Provisions

Now that you know your way around the "meat" of a contract, let's take a look at some of the bones: the boilerplate language. Boilerplate language refers to the many provisions at the end of the contract that are generally "standard" for most agreements of a particular type. On your cable or cell phone services agreements, for example, there is probably some small print at the bottom that you never read but is the most likely to get you into a world of trouble. That small print is considered boilerplate language. While slightly less important than the "meat" of a contract, boilerplate language is still significant to the overall protection provided by a contract. Accordingly, you should at least be familiar with the terms normally found in the boilerplate section. I'm not expecting you to read this and then go challenge your landlord about the indemnification provision (or lack thereof) in your most recent lease agreement. However, if a conversation ever comes up about it, you will hopefully be able to follow along and not completely space out. Once that conversation ends, I would highly recommend that you seek out your lawyer for advice. If someone is attempting to negotiate indemnity clauses with you, it's probably time to bring out the big guns.

Indemnification

Indemnity is one party's request to another party for compensation for any loss or damage suffered as a result of the other party's actions (generally towards third parties) arising out of the contract. For example, let's say you hire a photographer to take pictures for you at your event as an independent contractor. During the event, the photographer accidentally knocks over an old lady and breaks her hip. If the old lady sues you for the photographer's battery because it was your party, you can demand that the photographer *indemnify* you for all costs you incur defending the lawsuit against the old lady. The photographer may not have the money to reimburse you for those costs, but if you have a valid indemnification clause in your agreement, you will have the right to go after him to recoup your losses.

Indemnification provisions can be reciprocal, meaning both parties will have to reimburse the other for losses; or they can be unilateral, meaning: one party will be responsible for all loss or damage under a contract. Try to make sure that at worst, both parties receive indemnification and at best, you alone receive indemnification.

Picture This: a sample indemnification clause may look something like this (the following is a unilateral indemnification provision):

"Party A shall indemnify, defend, hold harmless and be liable to Party B for any claim, lawsuit, demand, or loss (which term shall include claims of or payments to third party claimants, attorney's fees and all other costs incurred in investigation of claims, negotiation of settlements and litigation) brought against, sustained or incurred by Party B arising out of any material breach by Party A of any representation or warranty contained herein or

out of any of the services contemplated
hereunder including, but not limited to fraud,
defalcation, dishonesty or misappropriation,
loss or misapplication of funds, intentional acts
or omissions or any other loss resulting from a
violation of this Agreement."

Governing Law and Venue

Governing law and venue are often grouped together
in the same provision. The governing law provision of a
contract sets forth what state's laws will govern the
contract in the event of dispute or litigation. Venue
specifies the state and/or court system that either party
will have to file suit in, in the event of litigation. Be sure
to choose a state where it would be convenient for you to
bring forth or defend against a lawsuit. It would be awful
to have to try and file a breach of contract claim in
Timbuktu when you live in Kansas. However, if the venue
provision in your contract says that all litigation arising
out of the contract must be filed in Timbuktu, then
Timbuktu is where you shall file suit.

 Picture This: A sample governing law and
venue provision may look like this:

"This Agreement shall be governed by and
interpreted and construed in accordance with

the laws of the State of Timbuktu, without regard to its conflicts of law provisions. For purposes of litigating any dispute that arises directly or indirectly from this Agreement, the parties hereby consent to the exclusive jurisdiction of the State of Timbuktu and agree that such litigation shall be conducted only in the courts of St. Nowhere, Timbuktu, or the federal courts of the United States for the Northern District of Timbuktu, and no other courts."

Notice

The notice provision tells you (1) where, (2) how and (3) to whom you should deliver important or official communications to the other party about the contract. This provision is extremely important because if you don't deliver notice to the other party in a way deemed acceptable by this provision, your notice may not be considered delivered to and/or received by the other party.

For example, let's pretend the notice provision of your agreement requires you, "to send the other party 30-days written notice via standard mail for the notice to be considered sufficient." You then decide to terminate the agreement and need to send the other party notice of your decision. If you send the other party an email when the notice provision required you to send a letter via standard mail, your notice will be considered insufficient and you won't have delivered proper notice to terminate the agreement.

It is also important to include updated contact information in the notice provision of a contract. You want to make sure that the place where you instruct a party to send you notice is a place where you will actually receive it. You also want to make sure you are sending your notices to the right person/place. Further, you can and should provide several different methods for acceptable delivery of notice such as fax, e-mail, standard mail or certified mail. If you do provide options, make sure you include proper contact information for each option provided.

Picture This: A sample notice provision may look like this:

"Any notice required or permitted to be given under the terms of this Agreement shall be sufficient if in writing and if sent postage prepaid by United States registered or certified mail, return receipt requested; by hand delivery, confirmed telecopy (facsimile), or electronic mail, to the following designated representative(s) of the parties (or such other parties as subsequently designated by the parties hereto in writing) at the following addresses (or such other address as may be subsequently designated to the parties hereto in writing):

IF TO PARTY A: Name of Party A
Party A Rep
Party A Address
Party A e-mail
Party A fax number

IF TO PARTY B: Name of Party B
Party B Rep
Party B Address
Party B e-mail
Party B fax number"

Automatic Renewal

Always be on the lookout for these! They will get you if you're not careful. Automatic renewal provisions automatically renew the term of an agreement. This means that you must actively terminate the agreement for it to end as opposed to the agreement expiring or coming to a natural end at the conclusion of the term. This provision is dangerous because if you're not careful, your agreement could automatically renew forever. I do not recommend automatic renewal provisions in agreements. Even if the agreement is between you and a very valuable partner, there is no harm in allowing the original contract to end and executing a new contract upon expiration of the original term. Executing a new contract gives everyone an opportunity to re-evaluate the terms of the agreement and to make sure they are still advantageous for all parties. However, depending on your product/service, automatic renewal provisions could be quite advantageous for your business.

 Picture This: An automatic renewal provision may look something like this:

> "Upon expiration of the initial term, this agreement shall automatically renew for successive one (1) year terms unless otherwise terminated by either party in writing at least thirty (30) days prior to any renewal term."

Assignment

An assignment is a transference of rights or interest in a contract from one party to another. It is when one party "signs away" their rights to a contract to someone else. Why would someone want to give away their rights to a contract? Well, let's say I sell widgets and I have a contract to sell my widgets to a wholesaler for ten years. In year five of our contract, I decide to sell my widget business to my cousin and retire in the Caribbean. However, my wholesaler does not want to let me terminate our contract which is still active for five more years. If my contract allows for assignment, I can assign my rights under the contract to my cousin so that I am free to retire in Jamaica and the wholesaler still gets his widgets. Once the contract is assigned, the person and/or business entity which you assigned your interest to, becomes primarily liable under the contract. However, if they fail to perform, you may still retain some secondary liability.

Be advised: contracts do not have to allow assignment. Make sure to take note whether yours does or does not. Further, like indemnification, an assignment provision in a contract can be reciprocal or unilateral.

 Picture This: An assignment provision may look something like this:

"Party A shall not assign or otherwise transfer or purport to assign or otherwise transfer this Agreement or any of its rights or obligations hereunder or any part hereof without the prior consent in writing of Party B, except that Party B may assign any of its rights or obligations to an affiliate, and Party B shall further have the right to assign this Agreement to an entity that acquires all or substantially all of its assets, all of the members' interests or equity in any form, or to an entity into which Party B is merged; provided, however, that Party B shall give Contractor prompt notice thereof, and the person or entity to whom the rights and obligations of Party B are assigned (the "Successor") shall execute a written instrument (in a form acceptable to Contractor) whereby the Successor agrees to accept all of the rights and obligations of Party B under this Agreement and agrees to be bound by all of the terms and conditions of this Agreement in the same manner as Party B."

STEP 8

GET PEOPLE:

INDEPENDENT CONTRACTORS and EMPLOYEES

By this point, I'm sure you're realizing that this, 'starting your own business' thing is A LOT of work. Running a business as a solopreneur or even with a partner or two is no small feat. Between setting up the business, managing day-to-day operations, marketing, servicing clients, handling finances and putting out fires, things can go from manageable to out of control REAL QUICK. When you get to the point that's just past perpetual exhaustion but not quite nervous breakdown, it may be time to consider hiring some help. But what's the best way to engage talent when you are starting a new business? Do you hire full-time employees? Part-time employees? Independent contractors? What is the difference between an employee and an independent contractor? How do I limit liability for independent contractors? For employees? This chapter will define and compare employees and independent contractors to help you determine which is a better fit for your business now and in the future.

Section 8.1 Independent Contractors
What is an independent contractor?

An independent contractor is a worker who contracts with individuals or entities to provide services in exchange for compensation. An independent contractor does not necessarily work regularly for any single company and is not an employee. The test for determining whether or not a person is an independent contractor versus an employee is: if the hiring company has the right to control or direct only the result of the work, not what and how the work will be done, then the individual is an independent contractor.

For example, if I hire a woman who provides cleaning services as an independent contractor to regularly perform maintenance on my office building, I may tell her what services I need and when I need them done. However, I should not tell her what equipment to use, what workers to hire or how to perform her cleaning services. Why? They and she are not my employees and thus, not under my direction or control. Also, note that an independent contractor can be an individual or company.

The following are some defining characteristics of independent contractors:

- Charges fees (i.e. flat, hourly, daily or weekly rates) for service
- Not limited in who they can work for/with (can work with several companies at the same time)
- Is engaged only for a limited amount of time, generally the time required to perform a service or task
- Retains control over the method and manner of work
- Is responsible for paying their own social security, Medicare and taxes
- Does not receive any benefits (medical insurance, liability insurance, retirement, paid time off…etc.)
- Receives a 1099 tax form instead of a W-2

What can I hire an independent contractor to do?

Contracting companies can hire independent contractors to perform ANY kind of service or fulfill any role including but not limited to: office assistant, virtual assistant, janitorial services, delivery persons, marketing director, CFO, lawyer, accountant, designer etc. As long as the contracting company treats the individual as an independent contractor for the duration of the relationship, independent contractors can be hired to perform any service the contracting company wishes them to perform.

What are my obligations to independent contractors?

The contracting company is only obligated to provide the independent contractor what is specified in the independent contractor agreement. Obligations of contracting companies in independent contractor agreements typically include the following:

- Payment
- Access to company files/information
- Deadlines

What is my liability for acts of independent contractors?

In most cases, contracting companies are not liable for the acts of independent contractors. Because independent contractors retain control over how their work is performed, and are not employees of the company, contracting companies are not usually held responsible for any negligent, illegal or unethical activities of independent contractors, even if the independent contractor engages in said activity while performing work for the contracting company.

Contracting companies CANNOT however, hire an independent contractor, call him/her an independent contractor and then treat him/her like an employee. Giving an independent contractor "employee treatment' can erode a company's limited liability for actions independent contractors engage in while performing work for or on behalf of the company. Treating an independent contractor as an employee can also open up the contracting company to various claims by the independent contractor like failure to provide: benefits, payment of taxes, overtime pay, liability insurance etc. The following are some ways that you (as a contracting company) can limit your liability when dealing with independent contractors:

- Execute an independent contractor agreement that clearly defines the worker as an independent contractor.
- Include an indemnification provision in your independent contractor agreement. (Revisit Section 7.2 for a refresher on indemnification provisions.).
- Limit your instructions to them on performance of work.

- Pay them a flat fee or an hourly rate vs. a salary.
- Do not provide training on how to perform their work. You can, however, educate them on the specifics of your business.
- Do not conduct formal evaluations of their work.
- Limit the number of expenses you pay on their behalf.
- Do not restrict their ability to work for others.
- Set a definite end date for the service. Do not allow the relationship to continue indefinitely.

How do you draft an independent contractor agreement?

Drafting an independent contractor agreement is similar to drafting other agreements. You must be sure to cover topics like term, termination, payment, the parties, indemnification, insurance, assignment, confidentiality and notice (See Chapter 6 How to Interpret a Contract for more details on how to draft these provisions). Two additional provisions that you should include in your independent contractor agreements are: (1) a relationship of the parties provision and (2) a schedule of services.

(1) **Relationship of the Parties Provisions.** Defining your relationship with the independent contractor is key to making it clear that your intent is to hire

and treat them as an independent contractor versus an employee.

Picture This: The following is an example of a Relationship Clause that clearly defines the relationship between the company and the independent contractor (notice how the first line is in all caps to emphasize its importance):

"THIS IS AN INDEPENDENT CONTRACTOR AGREEMENT THAT ESTABLISHES AN INDEPENDENT CONTRACTOR RELATIONSHIP BETWEEN THE PARTIES. NOTHING HEREIN SHALL BE DEEMED TO CREATE AN EMPLOYER/EMPLOYEE RELATIONSHIP BETWEEN COMPANY AND CONTRACTOR. Contractor understands and agrees that Company will not consider Contractor an employee. Contractor understands that Company will furnish to Contractor and the Internal Revenue Service a Form 1099 indicating non-employee compensation paid by Company to Contractor during any tax year. Further, Contractor shall indemnify and hold Company harmless from and against any and all liability, costs, expenses and damages which arise as a result of Contractor's acts or omissions."

(2) **Schedule of Services.** Limiting/defining the scope of an independent contractor's services is another tool meant to further define the relationship between the contracting company and

independent contractor. It also helps to limit the company's liability for acts of the independent contractor. When drafting this section of an independent contractor agreement, it is often easier to include the scope of services as an attachment to the larger contract called a schedule, rather than including it in the body of the agreement. One reason why it makes more sense to attach a separate schedule is that sometimes the list of services is long and complicated. Another reason is, if you are utilizing a contract template that you will use over and over, it is much easier to remove schedules than it is to re-draft a large portion of the contract every time you use it for different contractors.

Advantages of Hiring Independent Contractors

- Limited liability for actions of independent contractors
- Do not have to cover an independent contractor's expenses for materials, equipment and/or supplies
- Not responsible for providing benefits such as medical, retirement, overtime or paid leave
- Not responsible for paying taxes, social security or Medicare

- Duration of relationship is limited to the time it takes to complete services
- You can hire a specialist or expert who is highly skilled at performing a specific task
- An independent contractor can include a whole team of people instead of just one employee
- Not required to provide any training and only limited instruction

Disadvantages of Hiring Independent Contractors

- Cannot limit who they work for and with. Independent contractors can work with many other companies including competitors
- Independent contractors can be expensive. Because independent contractors can be paid on a per project or hourly basis there is no cap on how much you may end up paying them. Whereas, you can cap an employee's wages by providing them a salary or limiting the number of hours they can work during a pay period.
- May not be able to develop a lasting relationship with an independent contractor like you could a long-term employee
- Limited control over how the independent contractor completes the work
- Potential liability for treating an independent contractor like an employee

Section 8.2 Employees

What is an employee?

An employee is a person who elects to be bound in the

service of another in exchange for money and other valuable consideration, where the employer has the right to control and direct the employee in the material details of how the services are to be provided. An employee is a single person or individual and cannot be a corporation or other business entity.

There are generally two kinds of employees: full-time and part-time. Full-time and part-time employees can be difficult to classify, however, because they are defined differently depending on the context of the conversation. For example, for purposes of calculating overtime pay, an employee is considered full-time if he/she works 40 hours per week. However, for the purpose of determining whether or not an employee is entitled to employer-provided health insurance benefits, a full-time employee is an employee who works for 30 hours or more per week or 130 hours or more per month (if the employee has an irregular schedule). Be sure to check with the Department of Labor to ensure that you are properly classifying employees and providing them with the required number of benefits based on their status as either part or full time.

What are my obligations to employees

Employers have many more obligations to employees

than they do to independent contractors, and employers are obligated to provide more benefits for full-time versus part-time employees. Some of the legal obligations employers have to employees are as follows:

- Provide a minimum wage
- Provide safe working conditions
- Provide workers' compensation insurance
- Pay taxes (social security, Medicare and unemployment) and health insurance (health insurance only required for full-time employees)
- Additional compensation (time and a half) for hours worked in excess of 40 hours/week (overtime)
- Up to 12 weeks of unpaid sick leave for certain medical situations of the employee or an immediate family member of the employee (for employees who have worked for the employer for at least 1250 hours over the previous 12-month period at a company with at least 50 employees)

Employers may provide additional benefits to employees like the following but are not required to do so:

- Paid breaks/meal times
- Retirement or pension plans
- Stock options
- Paid vacations
- Sick days
- Life insurance
- Disability insurance
- Fringe benefits

What is my liability for acts of employees?

Employers are responsible for most all acts (even if those acts were negligent or not expressly sanctioned by an employer) committed by employees through a legal theory known as respondeat superior. The English translation for respondeat superior is: "Let the master answer for the servant."

Respondeat superior requires that an employer be held legally responsible for the wrongful acts of an employee if such acts occur within the scope of the employment. Typically, when respondeat superior is invoked, the injured party will look to hold both the employer and the employee liable for the employee's wrongful acts. To limit your liability to third parties for the acts of employees, it is best to maintain a comprehensive liability insurance policy that covers your acts as well as the acts of your employees and implement strict policies to govern employee behavior.

How do you draft an employment agreement?

Employer/employee relationships can be express or implied. A relationship that is communicated expressly is one that has been reduced to writing in the form of a contract. A relationship that is communicated impliedly is one that is communicated through the actions and behaviors of the parties.

This means that you do not have to execute an employment agreement for an employee/employer relationship to exist. Mere treatment of a person as an employee will entitle them to certain rights as an employed person whether you have an agreement in place or not. If you elect to use an employment agreement for your employees, consider including the following:

- Payment
- Benefits (paid/unpaid leave, insurance, pension...etc.)
- Perquisites (company-provided cell phone, laptop, meals, out of state travel, mileage...etc.)
- Termination
- Work schedule
- Reporting structure
- Job title/duties
- Work-for-hire (if the employee will be creating intellectual property as part of his/her job)
- Confidentiality
- Non-compete (check your state laws for non-compete provision requirements)

If you elect not to use a formal employment agreement to hire employees, you should at least extend to each employee an offer letter that they must sign and return to accept employment. An offer letter can be short (one page) and to the point but should at least include:

- The employee's full name
- The employee's job title
- A brief description of the job duties/responsibilities
- The person to whom the employee will report
- Salary and benefits offered as a result of employment
- Employment start date
- The type of employment (at-will or term employment)
- If employment will be for a defined period of time, include the term of employment
- Information detailing how the offer can be accepted or declined
- A deadline for when the offer will expire

Finally, regardless of whether you decide to implement contracts for your employees, you should: (1) create policies/manuals for employees; (2) provide each new employee with a copy of the policies/manuals; and (3) have each new employee sign a statement saying that he/she has received and read the policies/manuals. The following is a list of policies that every business should have in place for its employees:

- Sexual harassment
- Disciplinary
- Nondiscrimination

- Ethics and Conduct
- Internet/Social media
- Safety
- Compensation/Benefit
- Confidentiality/Sensitive Data Maintenance

Advantages of Hiring Employees

- You have direct control over the work being done
- You can develop a more long-term, stable relationship
- You can prevent an employee from working for/with competitors
- You can place a cap on earnings by implementing a salary or hours cap

Disadvantages of Hiring Employees

- You retain full liability for wrongful acts committed by employees within the scope of their employment
- Must pay taxes, liability insurance, workers compensation insurance, unemployment and health insurance (for employees who work more than 30 hours per week)
- Must pay overtime (time and a half) for employees who work more than 40 hours per week
- Will have to provide some benefits
- Will have to provide training and/or continuing education

- Can be more difficult to terminate an employee/employer relationship than independent contractor relationships even if the employee is at-will

Employee vs. Independent Contractor Comparison Chart	
Employee	**Independent Contractor**
Direct control over manner of work	Limited control over manner of work
Paid a salary or hourly rate	Paid a flat fee per service (or per hour, week or month depending on the type of service)
Entitled to certain benefits	Entitled to no benefits
Receives a W-2 Tax Form	Receives a 1099 Tax Form
Can be one individual person	Can be an individual or a business
Can limit ability to work with other companies	No limit to who independent contractor can work for/with
Must provide a minimum wage	No minimum wage
Employment agreement or evidence of employee/employer relationship	Independent Contractor Agreement

Just So You Know: Because there is less risk in hiring an independent contractor, it is recommended for most new business to hire independent contractors instead of employees.

Hiring a person as an independent contractor is also a good way to do work with someone without having to make any lasting commitment to him/her. If you find that someone's services as an independent contractor are invaluable to your business and you want to "lock them down," you can always extend an offer of employment and hire him/her as an employee.

STEP 9

GET PAID:

CLIENT AGREEMENTS, INVOICES AND TAXES

Finally, we have made it to the portion of the book where we get to talk about the most important part of running a business…. making money! Unfortunately, I won't be telling you how to make money, but I will share with you some legal strategies to help you protect it with client agreements, properly drafted invoices and basic tax information. And when I say basic, I mean one step above saying, 'go hire an accountant ASAP'.

I know, not what you wanted to hear. But, that's all I got. If you want money-making lessons, you'll have to go pick up Mark Cuban's book.

Section 9.1 Client Agreements

If you are a freelance writer, creator, accountant, lawyer, virtual assistant or any other kind of service provider, you will have clients. If you have clients, then you need to have them sign a client agreement. Client agreements are binding, legal documents that define the relationship between a service provider and service consumer or client. They are valuable tools for helping you SECURE THE BAG. I know what you're thinking, "My clients love me. My clients trust me. They would never try to stiff me." Hey, maybe you're right, but maybe you're not. Why chance it? A client agreement won't guarantee that you get paid, but people are far less likely to not pay for something if they've signed a legally binding agreement promising to pay. Plus, having an agreement in place will serve as excellent evidence in the unfortunate event that a job or project results in litigation.

When it comes to drafting, client agreements should be comprehensive and all-inclusive. However, they should also be simple and relatively easy to understand. A client agreement should be no more than one or two pages. If you need to include more comprehensive terms, consider drafting general terms and conditions that are attached to every client's agreement. You don't want to deter potential clients from purchasing your service(s) by hitting them with a 10-page document fraught with legalese and hidden conditions.

Lastly, above all else, a good client agreement should do three things: (1) explain and define the services that *the client* will receive; (2) explain and define the payment that *you* will receive; and (3) explain and define what happens if either of you fail to perform (1) or (2).

(1) Schedule of Services Provision

A schedule of service(s) provision is a detailed description of the service to be provided to a client under a client agreement. It can be included in the body of the agreement or referenced in the agreement and included as a separate attachment if services are lengthy or complicated. This section will generally vary from client to client and job to job. Accordingly, it is best to leave this section of the agreement blank and fill it in once you have agreed upon terms of service with your potential client.

A good schedule of service is extremely detailed and provides a COMPLETE list of ALL services to be performed. Whatever you put in the Schedule of Service(s) is what you are obligated to do. To ensure that the client gets exactly what he/she wants and that you aren't required to do more than the client deserves, be sure to be thorough in your description of services. To help illustrate this concept, the following are some examples of good descriptions of services:

SCHEDULE OF SERVICES EX. 1:

I (freelance writer) will write for you (client) a fifteen hundred (1500)-word blog post on the mechanics of blogging for your website: www.bombblogs.com, to be delivered no later than three (3) days after the execution of this agreement. I will deliver to you two versions of the post: 1) a version compatible with Microsoft Word; and 2) a version compatible with your website's blogging platform, Blog Perfect.

SCHEDULE OF SERVICES EX. 2

Company will perform the following grooming services for your dog, Mr. Snuggles:

- Shampoo and Condition Coat
- Blow Dry Hair
- Trim Nails
- Manicure Paw Pads
- Facial Trimming
- Sanitary trim of private areas
- Flea and tick treatment.

(2) Payment Terms

Structuring terms of payment that are agreeable for both you and your client is key to getting paid for the work that you do. The following are several different payment structures to be considered when drafting client agreements.

Lump Sum

A lump sum payment is a single payment of money due at one time. Lump sum payments can become due at any time during your arrangement but are generally due either prior to the start of work or at the time work is completed.

Installments

Installments are payments that are due over a defined period of time versus being due at one time. The term of installments can include as little as two payments and as many as thousands of payments. There is no minimum or maximum number of payments required in an installment plan. Further, the term (period of time) over which payments are due can last as long as you wish. However, I would not recommend extending installment payments beyond the time it takes to complete the service. Completing the service prior to receiving payment in full, greatly reduces your chances of being paid. I know that you want to be flexible in allowing your customers to pay over time, but remember, the point of this whole chapter and your business is to GET PAID.

Finally, installment provisions are generally attached to the client agreement separately in the form of a schedule. Installment payment schedules should include the following:

- the date of first and last payment,
- the amount owed for each payment,
- the date of each payment,
- where/how each payment can be made, and
- any fee increases for late payments.

Deposits

A deposit is a sum, payable as a first installment on the purchase of goods and/or services or as a showing of good faith under a contract, the balance being due and payable at a later time. You should require that the first installment (deposit) of your payment plan be paid prior to the start of any work being performed. Deposits are not required for installment plans but are recommended as a show of good faith that your client is serious about paying your fees.

The amount required as a deposit is 100% at your discretion. However, deposits are generally 50% or less of the total amount owed. If you are interested in seeking more than 50% of your fees upfront, it may be best to require payment in full upfront. Once a deposit is paid, the remaining fees owed can be paid in one lump sum at a specified day/time or in installment payments over a period of time.

There are two types of deposits: 1) refundable and 2) nonrefundable. A refundable deposit is one that may be requested back by the customer for whatever reasons stated in your client agreement. To limit frivolous refund requests, I would recommend limiting reasons for refunds to legitimate dissatisfaction with goods and/or services. A nonrefundable deposit is one that will not be returned to the customer under any circumstances.

WARNING: If you decide to use a refundable deposit, do not, I repeat, DO NOT spend the deposit until after service has been rendered. Hold the money in escrow until all services are complete to the satisfaction of the client. Because the money is refundable, you want to make sure that you have the money ready and

available for return in the event the
customer requests a refund.

 Picture This: The following are
some sample payment provisions:

Lump Sum

I promise to pay for the Services, by
paying the full amount of
[$ _____] on [DATE OF
PAYMENT DATE] in full satisfaction
of any fees owed under this
Agreement.

Installment/Deposit

I promise to pay for the Services, by
paying the sum of [$ _____]
today, prior to the start of the Services.
I understand that the next payment of
[$ _____] is due on [DATE
OF PAYMENT DATE]. Subsequent
installments in the amount of [$
_____] will be paid on the
same day of each succeeding
[WEEK/MONTH/YEAR] until the
entire amount has been paid in full. A
complete payment schedule has been
attached to this Agreement as Schedule
A and is hereby included into this
Agreement by reference.

(3) Consequences for breach of agreement.

If either you or your client fail to uphold the promises you made to one another in the agreement, the client agreement should state the consequences each of you will face for breach of the agreement. Consequences for breach of contract are necessary for both parties. For without any consequence, there is little incentive to do the right thing. The following are some potential consequences that you should consider including in your client agreements:

Consequences for client breach (failure to pay)

- Late fees
- Discontinuation of service(s)
- Termination of the client agreement
- Litigation

Consequences for service provider breach (failure to deliver services)

- Withholding of payment
- Termination of agreement
- Litigation

- Diminished relationship with client

Just So You Know: Until it is signed, a client agreement is an open offer to perform the listed services. This means that the offer can still be accepted to form a binding legal agreement at any time. Accordingly, you do not want to keep an offer for your service open forever. To avoid this, be sure to include an expiration day/time at the bottom of the agreement. Thirty (30) days is a reasonable amount of time to leave an offer for services open. If a potential client elects to purchase your service(s) after the date of expiration, draft a new agreement and have he/she sign the updated contract. This will give you an opportunity to re-evaluate and update the agreement, if necessary, prior to having the potential client sign it. Think about it. You don't want someone turning up two years later with a freshly signed contract expecting you to perform services that you may or may not still perform at prices that may be inconsistent with your current price structures.

Section 9.2 Invoices

An invoice is a list of goods/services that includes the total cost for said goods and/or services. In other words, an invoice is a bill. Once a client or purchaser is presented with an invoice, it establishes an obligation on the part of the client or purchaser to pay. Invoices serve two key purposes: (1) they provide notice to your client that he/she owes you money; and (2) they provide you with a record of all monies paid or still outstanding. Because invoices serve as great records of payments, you should draft and issue an invoice to EVERY client you serve, even the ones who pay upfront. Once an invoice is paid, you should write "paid" on it and make one copy for yourself and one for the client. It will provide you with a record and your client with a receipt.

There are no strict rules on how to draft invoices, but a good invoice should include the following:

- An itemized list of goods/service(s)
- The price for each good/service (including tax, if any)
- Any discounts given for the goods/services
- The date the invoice was issued
- An invoice number
- The name, address and phone number of the client
- The name, address and phone number of the company
- Payment due date and when a payment will be considered late
- Consequences for late payments
- Methods of payment accepted
- Details of how payment can be delivered

- If you charge clients by the hour, include the total number of hours worked and the number of hours required to perform each service

Section 9.3 Taxes

Taxes are awful, like that huge pimple that you get smack dab in the middle of your forehead right before a big date that just won't leave no matter how much you try to pop, rub or wish it away. No matter what you do, taxes are the pimple you can't avoid. I am not going to discuss taxes in depth. There is NO replacement for the guidance and counsel of a good accountant. He/she will not only keep your butt out of jail, but he/she may also save you some money and help keep you organized along the way. Bottom line, if you are going to do business, you need to have or consult with an accountant. In the meantime, here are some answers to some basic tax questions to help build your tax acumen.

What is an Employer Identification Number (EIN)?

An EIN is a federal tax identification number for businesses. It is essentially a social security number for your business. It allows the government to keep track of your business and all of its commercial activity. You need to apply for an EIN as soon as you register your business with the secretary of state. You can obtain an EIN by filing an application online with the IRS at www.irs.gov.

What is sales tax?

Sales tax is a direct tax on consumption that many states and municipalities impose on the purchase of goods and/or services. Sales taxes are collected at the point of sale. Merchants and service providers are responsible for collecting the tax and submitting it to the state and/or municipality where the tax is owed. Every state has varying tax laws. You will need to review your individual state's tax laws for more information regarding the laws imposed by your state and your obligations, as a business owner, to pay said tax.

Some states: Alaska, Delaware, Montana, New Hampshire and Oregon do not have a sales tax. All other states have some form of sales tax. The amount of sales tax you pay is calculated as a percentage of the sales price of the good or service. If the sales tax is not passed to the consumer, the merchant or service provider will be forced to eat that cost and pay that price.

What is income tax?

Income tax is a tax imposed on all income received from any source by an individual or business entity. Simply put, income tax is the tax you pay based on how much you make. However, your actual income may be very different from your taxable income. For example, your actual income includes every penny your business earns during a period of time. Whereas, your taxable income is your actual income less any deductions.

What is a business deduction?

A business deduction is an expense of your business that you can use to reduce your taxable income. For example, if you made $100 in gross sales for your business, but spent $30 on employee salaries, $20 on materials and $10 on rent for your office, totaling $60 in expenses, you can deduct the $60 in expenses from the $100 in gross income to bring your taxable income from $100 to $40. This means you only have to pay tax on the $40 instead of the full $100.

The goal when calculating taxable income is to bring your gross income (amount of money earned before taxes or deductions are subtracted) down as much as possible by deducting all of your business expenses. Be advised, however, that not all expenses of your business are considered tax deductions and there are limits for how much of an individual expense can be deducted from income. The following are some of the expenses that can be used as deductions to reduce your business' taxable income:

- The cost of raw materials
- The cost of labor
- Employee salaries
- Cost of storage
- Cost of office space
- Business start-up costs
- Any improvements made to the business
- If you have a home-based business, you can deduct percentages of your mortgage interest, insurance, repairs, utilities and depreciation
- The cost of mileage on your car when used for business purposes
- Insurance

How often should I file taxes for my business?

As an individual, you are only required to file your

taxes once a year (in April). As a business, you should file your taxes quarterly in March, June, September and December. Depending on which state you're in and the nature of your business (goods vs. services), you may have to file your taxes on a monthly versus quarterly basis. Regardless of your quarterly or monthly tax filing requirements, you will still have to reconcile your personal taxes on an annual basis.

STEP 10

GET YOUR TOOLS READY:

NEW BUSINESS RESOURCE GUIDE

When I started my business, I didn't know, what services I needed, where to find service providers or how to choose between the thousands of service providers I discovered during random, late-night Google® searches. As a result, I ended up spending and indulging in more services than I actually used. Because the purpose of this guide is to make your new business journey a little bit easier, I have compiled a list of resources that will surely be of use to you at some point during your journey. No, I have not been paid to endorse or advertise any of these service providers (I wish I had), and there are many others out there. However, there is strength and comfort in a personal recommendation. All of the resources below were either recommended to me by someone else or have been used by me at some point during my entrepreneurial journey. Take my recommendations, however, with a grain of salt. My business may be different from yours. The tools that I need may be different from the tools that you will need. There is no one-size fits all category of business ownership. As a result, this list is by no means inclusive of every service provider necessary for every make and model of business, but this guide will undoubtedly serve as a great starting point for your research.

Section 10.1 Websites, Email Addresses and Domains

There are many different elements of website design. For example, you will need a domain name (the address for your site, a web host (the platform that houses your site and provides the tools necessary for it to be viewed on the internet), a template (a tool to help you build your site) and email addresses with the same .com address as your website.

*Side note: YES, you need an email address with the same .com address as your website. Having a Gmail® or

Yahoo® address for your business is very unprofessional. How would you feel if you asked the CEO of Snapchat® for a business card and his email address read ceoofsnapchat@gmail.com? You would assume that his business was low budget and illegitimate. Don't be THAT guy. Spend the extra money and get the professional yourname@yourbusiness.com address. Ok, rant over. Back to your regularly scheduled programming.

Domain registration platforms can provide you with all of the aforementioned services and more. You can use one platform for everything or several platforms for different purposes. The following is a list of platforms you can explore:

- **GoDaddy®** – GoDaddy® is literally a one-stop shop for all of your small business needs. You can purchase e-mail addresses, website domains, website templates, Microsoft® Office… you want it; they got it. However, being a jack of all trades makes you a master of none. And, because of the extreme convenience they provide, GoDaddy® can be very expensive.

- **Wix®** – Wix® is a website building tool with both free and paid options. It's very user-friendly and it can be free. But again, you get what you pay for. For example, if you select the completely free version of the tool, the word "Wix" will be included in your URL.

- **HostGator®** – Host Gator® is very similar to GoDaddy® but they offer a few less additional services, and their prices can be a tad more affordable. They are also a great tool if you have an e-commerce business (meaning you plan to sell products directly on your website).

- **Google® Domains** – Google® does everything. Of course, they offer domain registration services as well.

- **SquareSpace®** – SquareSpace® is a user-friendly, reasonably priced tool that walks you through the website creation process from domain registration to launch. If you have an eye for design and want to try to navigate the website creation process alone, try SquareSpace®.

- **Wordpress®** – Yes, you read correctly, Wordpress®. Wordpress® isn't just for blogging anymore. You can purchase a domain name and build a professional website using one of Wordpress®' many templates. The downside to Wordpress® is that it is not very user-friendly. It's typically used by more experienced designers and coders.

Section 10.2 Logos, Graphics and Custom Images

In the digital age, content is king. Here are some tools that will help you create great content (photos, graphics, blogs, social media posts etc.) for your business

- **Canva®** – Canva® is a great, free tool if you have an eye for design. It is a platform that allows you to create your own, professional-looking content and write your own rules. However, if you are not great at designing and need some help, Canva® may not be the platform for you.

- **Fiverr®** – Fiverr® is a platform where designers, writers, editors, freelancers etc. can advertise their services. Services can range in price from $5 to thousands of dollars depending on the service requested, and service types can range from logo design to promo video creation. The best part about Fiverr® is that with pricing starting as low as $5, you can try a few assorted designs/designers until you find one that works for you.

- **99 Designs®**- 99 Designs® is more expensive than Fiverr®, but it is a one-stop shop for a lot of different services. The quality/originality of the work and the quality of service tends to be higher as well (get what you pay for).

- **Taste of Ink** – If you have an idea for a business card, Taste of Ink will bring it to life. Literally, whatever you can dream up, they will make. However, that kind of flexibility comes at a steep price.

Section 10.3 Virtual Assistants

Need someone to answer your phones and

schedule your appointments but want the flexibility of a virtual office? Then consider hiring a virtual assistant. Virtual assistants give your business a super professional touch without the hassle of having to manage a physical person or office. If you want the freedom to operate your business from anywhere, virtual assistants are the way to go.

Most virtual assistant companies are very similar and offer varying plans at varying price points based on your company's level of need. You can increase your level of service as your business grows so that you are only paying for the services you need as you need them. You can't go wrong with any one of the following:

- Zirtual
- Ruby Receptionists
- Task Bullet
- Upwork®

Section 10.4 Virtual Business Phone Lines

You need a phone number for your business, but you don't want to use your personal cell number and you're not ready to invest in a separate phone? That's okay; you don't have to! There are plenty of business phone lines that will allow you to run your business right from your personal cell phone.

- **Free Services**

  - **Google® Voice** – Google® Voice is a free service if you only wish to *receive* calls from your Google® Voice number. Google® Voice will charge extra if you want to make outgoing calls as well. Google® Voice also allows you to text customers and will forward your text conversations directly to your Gmail® email account, if you have one.

- **Paid Services**

  All of the following services do virtually the same thing. Each has several paid options and functions as an app that allows you to operate two phone numbers on one phone. It works through your cellular service provider so you don't need wifi to operate it.

  - iPlum®
  - Line2®
  - eVoice®
  - GoDaddy® Smart Line
  - **Grasshopper®** – The best part about Grasshopper is that you can establish multiple phone numbers for your business. For example, you can make the "main line" for your business 505-555-0000 and then establish an extension for your "direct line" at 505-555-0000 ext. 101.

Section 10.5 Co-Working Spaces

Want to have the feel of going to work every day with a community of like-minded individuals without the price tag of an individual office space? Try a co-working space. Co-working is a style of workspace that involves a shared workplace, often in the form of a large open space with desks and chairs (similar to a library), and independent activity.

Some benefits of using co-working spaces are:

- Some spaces allow you to use the co-working space address as your company address, for a price.

- Most co-working spaces have conference rooms that you can use when you need to meet clients.

- For an extra fee, you can have your own space that is not shared by others.

- Starting a business by yourself can be lonely. A co-working space provides social interaction with other entrepreneurs. You can also do some great networking at co-working spaces. There are many fairly well-established companies that are housed in co-working spaces.

- Some co-working spaces offer receptionist services, for an extra fee.

- Co-working spaces are generally cheaper than traditional office spaces.

- If you only need the office on an occasional basis, some co-working spaces offer hourly, daily and weekly rates.

There are very few co-working spaces that operate on a national level. You will have to do some research to find out what co-working spaces are available in your city. However, some co-working spaces that operate in multiple cities are as follows:

- WeWork®
- TechSpace®
- Serendipity Labs®
- Industrious®
- ImpactHub®

Section 10.6 Business Banking

Unfortunately, the cost of doing business in 2018 is STEEP. For the most part, you can't even store your own money in a checking account without having to pay a fee. Most commercial banks offer accounts for new business owners at similar rates with similar services and options. However, if you are interested in free banking, the following are a couple of options you can explore to establish a simple business checking account without paying a monthly fee.

- **Spark® Capital One Business Account**. Capital One provides a 100% online account for small businesses that is 100% free. The upside is that it's free. The downside is that if you are the kind of person who needs to walk into a bank every now and again or if you deal with a lot of cash transactions, this may not be the best option for you.

- **Your local credit union**. If you are already a credit union member, you should be able to open a business account with your credit union. Credit unions typically require you to pay an initial investment fee but it's nominal ($25-$50) and you get it back when you close out the account. The best part is that outside of the initial investment fee, there are no future maintenance fees and you don't have to maintain a minimum account balance or do direct deposit to take advantage of the free account.

Section 10.7 Payment Processors

Unless you will require your customers to pay with cash, check or first-born children, you will need to establish a way to accept credit/debit card payments. You will want a payment processing company with reasonable processing fees, that is easy and user-friendly for you and your customers and integrates well with other platforms like your website and/or scheduling page. The following is a list of payment processors that are affordable, user-friendly and will make your business look extremely polished and professional to your customers.

- **Stripe®** - Stripe has great customization features that help you to customize the platform for your specific business needs. You can even accept Bitcoin as a form of payment using Stripe.

- **Square®** - the most unique feature about Square is that it has both online and POS capabilities. This is great for accepting payments in person.

- **PayPal®** - enough said.

- **Due** - If you provide services and like to issue invoices to your customers, Due is a platform that has invoicing and payment processing capabilities.

Section 10.8 Printing Services

Every new business needs great marketing tools. Some of the most effective marketing tools are still physical printed materials like business cards, flyers, pamphlets, brochures and newsletters etc. You can always check out your local print shop for printing services. However, I have found that online print services have greater capabilities and offer fancier options at lower prices. The following are some of the best online printing resources:

- **VistaPrint®** – VistaPrint provides reasonable quality printed materials with a fair amount of options at a reasonable price.

- **FedEx®, Kinkos®, Office Depot®** – The best feature of these traditional printing services is that they have physical stores to supplement their online platforms. Sometimes you just want to walk into a store, talk to a person and walk out with your materials.

- **Moo** – if you're looking for those super-thick high-quality cards, Moo is the best!

Section 10.9 Electronic Signature Tools

If you are a service provider with a contract-heavy business and you want to be paperless (and yes you do want to be paperless), you need electronic signature software. Let's face it. Who has time to print a client agreement, sign it, scan it and send it back? No one! And in with modern technology, why should you have to?

Before implementing an electronic signature tool, be sure to include an electronic signature provision in all of your agreements that states something similar to the following: "electronic signatures as applied to this document will be binding upon both parties and will have the same force and effect of an original signature." This language or something like it will ensure that your electronic signatures are valid and binding. Then, try one of the following vendors to make all of your paperless operating dreams come true:

- **DocuSign®** – DocuSign has a partnership with GoDaddy®. Accordingly, it is included for free in some of GoDaddy's® business user packages. If you are a GoDaddy® user, check to see if you already get free access to DocuSign®.

- **HelloSign®** - HelloSign® has a free option for low-volume users. This is a great way to test out the software before upgrading to a paid option.

- **AdobeSign®** - Formerly EchoSign®, AdobeSign® links with Adobe Acrobat® which makes it very user-friendly. It allows you to work with a platform that is very familiar to you because you are probably already using it. AdobeSign® also offers a WordPress® plug-in so you can incorporate it directly into your website.

Section 10.10 Business Management and Scheduling

When you are an entrepreneur, especially one with little to no staff, TIME IS MONEY. I'm sure you've heard this phrase before, but it takes new meaning when you are trying to run a profitable business. You will need time management and scheduling tools so that you can (1) make every second of your day count and (2) minimize the amount of time you spend on administrative tasks. This will allow you to focus your attention on fun things like creating, writing, selling or whatever makes your business run. The following are a list of tools that will help you do just that. And when I tell you that some of these tools literally changed my life, I'm not joking.

- **Acuity®** – Acuity® is a client appointment scheduling tool that allows clients to book their own appointments, pay their fees and fill out forms at their own time and convenience. It also sends follow up e-mails, appointment reminders and calendar invitations to both you and your clients. It offers both a free and paid option depending on your needs.

- **Calendly®** – Calendly® is another scheduling tool very similar to Acuity®. However, it is also a convenient tool for scheduling appointments and meetings internally with staff and team members as well as external customers and clients.

- **Convert Kit®** – E-mail is still the most effective tool for reaching your target customer. But who has time to sit down and send marketing e-mails? ConvertKit® is an e-mail marketing tool (similar to MailChimp which is also a GREAT and FREE tool) that will help you create, manage and distribute your e-mail marketing campaigns. Convert Kit® is especially recommended for e-commerce businesses.

- **Dubsado** – If you want to automate your life and have your business running on autopilot, Dubsado will have you functioning like a finely tuned automobile. Dubsado helps to streamline and automate various business processes including invoicing, payment, e-mail distribution, contracts, sales funnels and more.

- **asana®** – asana® is a project management tool that helps you focus your ideas and increase productivity.

Section 10.11 Community

There is absolutely no replacement for having a strong team of people in your corner. Entrepreneurship is not a journey you can take alone. You will need folks to support you, to cry with you, to celebrate with you and advise you. Accordingly, you will need to plug into some strong communities where you can find all of the above as well as some friends, mentors, cheerleaders and potential customers. One of the best ways to find these communities is through online support groups on Facebook and other social media platforms. The following is a list of some of my favorite online communities for entrepreneurs and small business owners.

- **BYOB Society** – The Build Your Own Brand (BYOB) society is an online community designed by millennial entrepreneurs for millennial entrepreneurs, creatives and young professionals to share ideas, tips and tricks for business, professional and personal development. They also host conferences and local-meetups so that community members can take their relationships offline. You can find them at their website or all major social media platforms including: Facebook, Twitter and Instagram.

- **#HERmovement** – The #HERmovement network is a dynamic community of over 2000 women entrepreneurs, creatives and side hustlers. The best part about the #HERmovement community is its unique focus on education. The group's administrator is a business development and branding guru who offers her classes, tips, guides and resources (sometimes for free), to community members. #HERmovement also has an annual conference where members can take their online relationships offline. You can find #HerMovement at their website or all major social media platforms including: Facebook, Twitter and Instagram.

- **Boss Lady, Esq.** – Boss Lady Esq. is an online Facebook community specifically designed for women law firm owners (sorry fellas). The group is unique in that ladies discuss all kinds of topics from selecting the perfect headshot for your website to which motions to file in a divorce dispute. The group also acts as a great referral source for its members and offers regular meet-up opportunities for ladies to connect offline.

- **LinkedIn®** – Do not sleep on the power of LinkedIn®. LinkedIn® is probably the MOST valuable tool you have in your community arsenal. Why? Because almost EVERYONE you want to know has one. A community is only as strong as its members and LinkedIn® includes just about anyone. It is also a safe, low pressure way to connect with and talk to people who you may not know in real-life but are interested in networking with for career advancement purposes.

- **Startup Nation** – Startup Nation has a little bit of everything. They provide great content through their blog, host a radio show, foster discussions on various topics through discussion boards, and provide resources for getting your business started. Startup Nation also offers a host of paid services all new businesses need. It is literally a one-stop-shop for all things Startup.

- **Small Business Administration**– The Small Business Administration (SBA) is an independent agency of the federal government created to aid, counsel, assist and protect small businesses. The best part of the SBA is that most of the services it offers are free and very useful. The SBA provides resources for obtaining small business loans, grants and federal funding. It also operates local district offices that you can visit in-person to speak with a representative or attend an SBA-hosted event.

Finally, the most valuable asset your business has is YOU. You are your business, especially in this phase of the game. Whatever time, energy, love etc., you exude will directly impact the health of your business. Be sure to bring your best every day so you can give your business your best every day. If you can do that, your business will have more than a fighting chance at survival.

References

The following is a list of materials that were referenced during the writing of 10 Steps to StartUP. Be sure to check out these resources for more information on any of the topics covered in this book.

Print Resources

P. Goldstein and R.A. Reese. *Unfair Competition, Trademark, Copyright and Patent Selected Statutes and International Agreements*. 2014

M. Chirelstein and L. Zelenak. *Federal Income Taxation Concepts and Insights.* 2015

R. Freer. *The Law of Corporations in a Nutshell*. 2016

M. LaFrance. *Copyright Law in a Nutshell*. 2011

Online Journal Resources

C. Meland and K. Jonas. *E-Commerce Payment Mechanisms*. 2018

G. Wirth. *Independent Contractor Classification*. 2015

Practical Law Intellectual Property & Technology by West Law. *Copyright Overview*. 2018

Practical Law Intellectual Property & Technology by West Law. *Trademark: Overview*. 2018

Practical Law Corporate & Securities by West Law. *Corporate Governance Practices: Commentary*. 2018

Practical Law Corporate & Securities by West Law. *LLC Agreement Commentary*. 2018

Practical Law Corporate & Securities by West Law. *Forming and Organizing a Corporation*. 2018

L. Jolly. *US Privacy and Data Security Law: Overview*. 2018

Website Resources

https://www.irs.gov/businesses/small-businesses-self-employed

https://www.uspto.gov/trademarks-getting-started/trademark-basics

https://www.uspto.gov/patents-getting-started/general-information-concerning-patents

www.copyright.gov

https://www.ftc.gov/tips-advice/business-center/guidance/how-comply-privacy-consumer-financial-information-rule-gramm

https://taxify.co/2016/11/16/business-risks-not-collecting-sales-tax/

https://www.sba.gov/business-guide

http://www.wpbeginner.com/beginners-guide/how-to-add-a-privacy-policy-in-wordpress/